UPSIDE-DOWN
LEADERSHIP

A ZOO VETERINARIAN'S JOURNEY
TO BECOMING A SERVANT LEADER

UPSIDE-DOWN LEADERSHIP

DON JANSSEN, DVM

Corporate Director, Animal Health
San Diego Zoo Global (retired)

SAN DIEGO ZOO GLOBAL PRESS

Praise for Don Janssen and
Upside-Down Leadership

"Students of servant leadership will say that influence is the key to being an effective leader. Since I was hired by Don in 1991 to join the veterinary team at the San Diego Zoo, I have benefitted from his tireless quest to find a leadership style that would work for his team. After years of study and reading dozens of references on the topic, Don eventually settled on servant leadership as the style he would carry forward through the rest of his career. Don's gentle, fair, respectful approach, along with his high intellect, extraordinary work ethic, and firm adherence to great values, made him extremely influential—not only at San Diego Zoo Global but regionally, nationally, and now internationally. A humble man by nature and a true servant leader, Don never set out to gain fame or recognition for his efforts but to provide a way to establish a safe, respectful, professional department where the team, the people working with the team, the animals, and the institution could thrive. Yet as a result of his servant leadership style, Don's influence grew almost exponentially to the point where today he is one of the most trusted veterinarians in zoo medicine. Now, Don is realizing his dream as the veterinary team at San Diego Zoo Global has transitioned into a new team empowered by a solid foundation in servant leadership principles. I will always be thankful to Don for teaching me and holding me accountable to be a servant leader. I highly recommend servant leadership to anyone who is placed in a position of management authority. As I have discovered in my career, Don's thoughts on the subject are well worth reading."

—Patrick J. Morris, DVM, DACZM Associate Director, Global Clinical Services, San Diego Zoo and San Diego Zoo Safari Park

"I encourage anyone who wants to become a better leader to read *Upside-Down Leadership*. Don masterfully weaves the key practices of servant leadership through stories from his incredible veterinary career. He inspires leaders from all walks of life to increase their influence and make a lasting difference."

—Robin Swift, President, Servant Leadership Institute

"My partnership with Don and the San Diego Zoo and Safari Park has been one of the most rewarding of my career. Talk to anyone who worked with Don and they will describe the behaviors of a servant leader who always remained humble, yet demonstrated courage to do the right things."

—Rodney Jackson, Executive Coach, Servant Leadership Institute

"Don has been an impactful mentor throughout my career, and I am grateful to have had the opportunity to work for him. Watching his leadership style evolve has been inspiring and encouraging. He has helped me to appreciate that leading is tough work, requiring study, self-awareness, reflection, forgiveness, and a sense of duty. Being a student of leadership is a lifelong journey, and I credit Don for leading me down this rewarding path. Don's unassuming nature, candor, and strong values are at the center of his leadership style as is his desire to serve and influence."

—Nadine Lamberski, DVM, Corporate Director of Animal Health, San Diego Zoo Global

Upside-Down Leadership: A Zoo Veterinarian's Journey to Becoming a Servant Leader was published by San Diego Zoo Global Press in association with Beckon Books. Through these publishing efforts, we seek to inspire readers to care about wildlife, the natural world, and conservation.

San Diego Zoo Global is committed to leading the fight against extinction. It saves species worldwide by uniting its expertise in animal care and conservation science with its dedication to inspire a passion for nature.

Douglas G. Myers, President and Chief Executive Officer
Shawn Dixon, Chief Operating Officer
Yvonne Miles, Corporate Director of Retail
Georgeanne Irvine, Director of Corporate Publishing

San Diego Zoo Global
P.O. Box 120551
San Diego, CA 92112-0551
sandiegozoo.org | 619-231-1515

San Diego Zoo Global's publishing partner is Beckon Books, an imprint of Southwestern Publishing Group, Inc., 2451 Atrium Way, Nashville, TN 37214. Southwestern Publishing Group is a wholly owned subsidiary of Southwestern/Great American, Inc., Nashville, Tennessee.

Christopher G. Capen, President, Southwestern Publishing Group
Betsy Holt, Publisher, Beckon Books
Kristin Connelly, Managing Editor
Vicky Shea, Senior Art Director/Interior Design
Scott Ramsey, Cover Design
swpublishinggroup.com | 800-358-0560

ISBN: 978-1-935442-69-1 (hardcover)
ISBN: 978-1-935442-70-7 (softcover)
Library of Congress Control Number: 2018933870

Printed in the United States
10 9 8 7 6 5 4 3 2 1

Contents

"I Quit"

The year I turned thirty, I landed my dream job as an associate veterinarian at what was then called the San Diego Wild Animal Park. Then in early 1987, as I turned thirty-five, I was given a job I never dreamed of having—the director of veterinary services at the San Diego Zoo.

Six months later, I quit.

As I walked back to the Zoo hospital from my boss's office after resigning that September morning, I unpinned my name tag from my shirt and took a final look at it: "Donald L. Janssen, DVM, Director, Veterinary Services." I stared hard at the tag's black-and-white giant panda–face emblem. We'd just received giant pandas on a short-term loan from China, which was the beginning of an international effort that was destined to turn into a conservation success. It was an exciting time to be at the San Diego Zoo. We could clearly see we were entering a new era. And I had the once-in-a-lifetime chance to play a leadership role in it.

There was only one problem. I'd been hired to navigate a long-standing dysfunctional staff situation, a malignant clashing of vision and personalities that was now threatening the health of the department, the animal care operation, and in some ways the entire Zoo. The Zoo's administration had tried many strategies without success. Even though I had no training in leadership principles and practices in my many years of schooling, I thought I could be the one to fix the situation. As a young boss, I was challenged at every step, but I thought I could handle it. With the help of my own boss, I had worked out overall expectations for my new department, focusing on openness, respect, and quality animal care. In fact, I'd just come back from a conference of the American Association of Zoo Veterinarians with innovative ideas to try.

That morning I'd gone into what we call "rounds discussion" with great hope. Instead, as we got into the meeting, the conflicts between my team members erupted.

Accusations and blame were flying around the room; no one was even attempting to be professional anymore. I realized, sitting there in the middle of the fight, the argument growing louder and louder, that I was not going to fix this problem. In fact, if I had to continue even one more day trying to manage these team members, I thought I'd explode. So as the team members continued squabbling, I got to my feet, walked to my boss's office, and quit. On my way back to my office to pack up and leave, I took a final look at my prized name tag. Then I tossed it in the bushes along the road.

That desperate moment, though, wasn't the end of the story. Instead, it became a turning point in my career.

I got a second chance.

That very afternoon my boss called me with the news that he and the executive committee had decided to suspend the entire veterinary and technician staff until they could decide what to do about the situation. He said he understood my reasons for giving up, but he asked that I come in the next day. The veterinary resident would be the only veterinarian left if I didn't, and she'd been there just a few months. So I came back. That day was the beginning of a multiyear rebuilding of the veterinary department and my personal education in effective leadership.

I soon found out that variations on this story were happening at other zoos around the country as well.

Why? I wondered.

The near-loss of my San Diego Zoo veterinary career would have been catastrophic for me personally, but it also would have represented the loss of influence in the zoo world by a profession with so much untapped value. In fact, just a generation or two ago, the world's top zoo directors had been veterinarians by training first and executives second. Now only rarely did a veterinary-trained executive lead a zoological organization.

Something big had changed.

Over the years, veterinary professionals had become compartmentalized, our specialized training forcing us into smaller and smaller niches of the zoological world's framework. The situation had created formidable obstacles between zoo veterinary professionals and influential leadership at their institutions' highest levels. That seemed not only a shame but also a waste for both veterinarians and institutions, not to mention its effect on the animals in our care.

Yes, something big had changed. But that didn't mean it couldn't change again for the better. So I became committed to finding an effective leadership dynamic that worked in the modern zoo veterinary world and then teaching it to other veterinary professionals.

In August 2016, thirty years after I quit my job, I retired, leaving the department in good hands. We'd grown from a tiny group of veterinarians and technicians to six veterinarians and six technicians plus a veterinary resident at both San Diego Zoo Global sites—the Zoo and the Safari Park (previously the Wild Animal Park). We oversaw two clinical laboratories, one at each site, with a total of eight technicians and a laboratory manager. We had a nutrition staff that included three PhD or MS nutritionists plus support staff. We'd also begun to have overall influence in the organization itself, and I'm very proud of that.

Easily, this could have turned out much differently. In fact, if not for a studied effort to turn the philosophical and practical dynamics of my personal leadership upside down, my story would have been just another variation of the same old story.

Libraries are filled with books on leadership. This leadership book is meant for the future leaders in the profession I love—zoo veterinary medicine—and for anyone who wants to gain influence in their organization. I am writing to those who feel called to grow their sphere of influence for the benefit of others and not for selfish ambition. It is a narrow road with challenging obstacles. But to those willing to face the challenge, I want to inspire, encourage, and guide you in this "upside-down" way to become a successful, influential leader in your own organization. I hope that you will be bold and courageous, using your influence to do what is right and just.

What I learned between that September day I quit and the August day I retired made all the difference in having a fulfilling and humbly influential career. My dream is that what I share in the following pages will do the same for you.

CHAPTER 1

The All-Too-Common Story

Veterinarians are among the most trusted and respected of all professionals, known for compassion and objectivity. We begin as animal lovers in our youth and find our way to the profession as a calling. The beginning of the veterinarians' oath expresses the profession's selfless nature:

> *I solemnly swear to use my scientific knowledge and skills for the benefit of society through the protection of animal health. . . .*

But in today's zoos, veterinarians are often perceived differently, in some cases maligned. Even as a young veterinarian entering the field of zoo medicine, I heard stories of veterinarians who were not allowed keys to animal enclosures and forced to go through supervisors just to talk to the keepers. It broke my heart to think of zoo veterinarians being sidelined like this. I witnessed the personal and professional toll it took on individuals who had chosen to dedicate their lives to taking care of zoo animals, many of which were species teetering on the brink of extinction.

What was the problem?

I began to ask that very question. And the responses were telling.

I heard about cases in which veterinarians were viewed solely as mechanics with technical tasks to complete. I heard about animal staffs that were intimidated by veterinarians' higher level of education. I heard about how veterinarians were overstepping their authority and becoming roadblocks for progress. I heard about arrogant veterinarians with "I'm the doctor and you're not" personalities. Finally, I heard from zoo directors who believed that veterinarians were overly specialized in their training and interests, isolated and insulated with little interest in the health of the organization as a whole.

Mechanics, roadblocks. Arrogant, isolated.

Does that sound harsh? Or does it have a ring of truth? How did such a group of noble, animal-loving, service-oath-taking professionals come to be described this way?

For me, the answer was a long time in coming. As a young manager tasked with rebuilding an entire veterinary department, I'd made the same crucial mistake over and over: I hired and trained people based on their individual achievements alone. In other words, I thought that the best zoo veterinarians would be the ones with the greatest technical skills and most career achievements.

I soon learned, however, that for zoo veterinarians to have true, long-standing success, they needed to have the leadership skills and temperament that supported collaboration. They needed to value the success of the team above their own success. This was very different from the usual guidelines for hiring and training. Frankly, it was very different from what zoo veterinarians themselves probably would see as the way to achieve success.

And that mentality, I believe, comes from an all-too-common story. The story goes something like this:

To achieve a career in zoo animal medicine, people follow a predictable path. Future veterinarians, who are usually among the brightest in their high school class, perform to a high individual standard in undergraduate college due to their abilities and diligent work habits. They develop mentor relationships to earn recommendations that set them apart from others. They sacrifice for years to complete their veterinary school education, followed by multiple internships to land a prestigious zoo medicine residency.

As zoo residents, they work long hours, learning to make life-and-death clinical decisions. At the same time, they are preparing research studies, writing for scientific publications, and studying for the comprehensive examination required to become board certified as a specialist in the American College of Zoological Medicine.

This extreme investment in time and money leads to a strong bond between people in the zoo veterinary profession. But although they have opportunities to develop teamwork and leadership skills, the vast majority of their time is focused on individual achievement. So when these young veterinarians become board certified, finally arriving at the pinnacle of their educational achievement, they believe their potential for career success ought to be limitless.

Here, the story often takes an unfortunate twist. Sadly, this long path of study and training often does not ensure the satisfying success that high-achieving new zoo veterinarians would hope. Despite all their hard work and new credentials, they do not obtain the influence and position they thought they would earn. They become disappointed and frustrated. Too often, such disappointment grows into dissatisfaction with their position and coworkers.

That's bad enough—but something larger is at stake.

Zoo veterinarians have a unique vantage point others in the zoo do not have. Not only do they function as animal welfare advocates, but they also have knowledge, experience, and a valuable perspective for influencing the direction of the organization. Furthermore, in their regulatory role, attending veterinarians provide credibility and legitimacy to their organization.

They have daily experience in complex decision-making. They are trained to ask questions and obtain histories that offer unique views of the whole picture concerning each animal care case.

In other words, their wealth of technical training and animal care expertise is not only necessary, it is foundational for any zoo to function. Is it any wonder that zoo veterinarians become disappointed when they lack influence over organizational decisions and strategic direction?

Zoo veterinarians' loss of influence within their larger organization is a tragic waste. When that influence is lost, it can lead to serious conflict with decision-makers and create long-standing battles of will. No one wins. And animal care is bound to suffer.

This all-too-common story occurring today in zoo veterinary medicine is likely taking place in other highly invested technical or professional careers as well. Traps and obstacles abound that keep the same story happening again and again.

It doesn't have to be this way.

What Is Organizational Influence?

If you had to choose between having power, authority, or influence in your career, which would you consider to be most fulfilling and effective in the long run?

If you chose anything but influence, you chose wrong.

Influence—not power or authority—brings the truest significance to a career. A recent Mayo Clinic study done on physician burnout showed that those who have influence and meaning at work are inclined to suffer less burnout and are more likely to have a satisfying career.

What is influence?

Influence is the elusive ability to make an impact on the thinking and actions of others without the need to exert control or authority. In fact, having influence does not require a position of authority. You don't need position, authority, or control to have influence. The opportunity to influence is available to anyone. Why? Because influence springs from a person's value to others. That is really the measure of effectiveness—your influence.

Veterinarians can have plenty of influence among their professional peers but none in the larger sphere of their zoo organization. How can this be? It's no doubt a head-scratcher to them. But it's true: having positional authority does not guarantee influence. In fact, it can get in the way of having broader organizational influence.

I began to understand why only after asking zoological leaders around the world for answers. I mentioned some of their feedback earlier. Here are a few of the most telling responses.

Self-Interest

- Many people stated that zoo veterinarians create their own obstacles to gaining influence in their organizations. One of the biggest self-created obstacles is being a prima donna, which causes problems with peer leaders. In fact, one responder pointed out that newly graduated veterinarians seem to "wear their degree on their forehead."

- Several people chose the word *arrogance*. One executive stated it this way: "Arrogance is seen in many veterinarians—either overt or subtle—if things don't go their way. To us, it becomes 'crying wolf.'" He went on to say, "Veterinarians are a viable part of the organization, but many veterinarians act as if they are the center."

- One CEO expressed concern that "veterinarians don't know how to listen and do not show an interest in people."

- "Many zoo veterinarians avoid dealing with conflict," said another. "They may just not have the interest in leadership or think they don't have anything of value to offer beyond their own animal care realm."

Obstacles

- Veterinarians become roadblocks by exerting their power as unique subject matter experts. Many responders expressed this problem.
- Some characterized the style of veterinarians as "black-and-white" and lacking in flexibility. One leader commented, "People who become veterinarians do so because they care about animals—and even have an oath. They come preselected not to compromise." A director said that he recently had a veterinarian draw a deep line in the sand over an animal acquisition. He said this type of rigid behavior undermines the practice of veterinary medicine in general: "The veterinarians' background—i.e., love of animals—conflicts with the general business balance. They do not acknowledge that the organization sustaining animals must stay healthy itself."
- This sentiment was echoed by several responders. Zoo veterinarians, they said, just don't seem to have business savvy and "appear resistant to the fact that we are running a business."
- As a result of these roadblock tendencies, executive leaders tend to shut veterinarians out of larger decision-making.

Priorities

- Another repeated theme was time and how to prioritize it. Several of the responders mentioned that simply being present at planning meetings was important but that veterinarians often miss these meetings, frequently offering the excuse that they had "a case to deal with." Whether their excuse is legitimate or not, their absence is an obstacle to developing influence. "You have to be at the table to have influence," said one director.
- This poor time management creates a self-defeating effect. "The veterinarians buy into an 'I'm disregarded' mind-set," said a responder.

"Then they feel powerless. It seems to stem from being so focused on the work and in a constant state of overwhelm, which keeps them from reaching out to the larger organization."

Perception of Veterinarians

- Several of those who responded acknowledged that there is another side to the coin. One observed a desire by the animal husbandry leadership to keep veterinarians out of decision-making because they feel "threatened by different perspectives or higher education." Another person stated it this way: "People put veterinarians in a box—they are supposed to take care of animals. It is hard to get people to think differently, and they often seem surprised to see veterinarians in leadership roles and not acting in the traditional clinical role."
- One farsighted CEO summed up the basic problem of differing perspectives: "Institutional management has a tendency to focus on strategy, while veterinary practice tends to focus on operational and individual cases. Without a strong shared value system to bridge this gap, different perspectives will lead to conflict."

As you might imagine, hearing all this was enlightening. But I didn't understand everything fully until I was part of the executive team myself. One day I got a call from my CEO asking if I would join the executive team. I would be the first clinical veterinarian ever to do so, he informed me. I'd already been in my position for years and had begun a study of leadership in earnest, looking for ways to improve leadership and strategy on the animal side of the Zoo. I quickly accepted, anticipating how much my animal care expertise could help the interests of the animals. But I soon learned that my motivation, albeit a good one, was not the best reason to be a part of the Zoo's executive team. I wasn't there solely to be an advocate for my department and its focus on animal health. I was there to view my expertise within the context of the entire institution and bring that knowledge to the table for the benefit of all.

In other words, I learned about organizational influence.

Organizational influence is the power to shape policy and affect organizational planning. It can be the catalyst for making the right things happen by cultivating trusting relationships with others in the same position. This ability to influence fellow decision-makers benefits the reputation of the person, the team, the department, the organization, and the entire profession.

My CEO had trusted I would rise to this understanding simply by being exposed to how the organization itself functioned and learning that it was essential for *all* departments to be healthy, not just my own. Surprising even myself, I became interested in strategic planning, financial reporting, messaging, human resources, fund-raising, operations, and construction. Why? Because I soon grasped that conservation and animal health were intimately connected to all those areas. The diversity of expertise and interests on the executive team was impressive, but the unity of purpose was key.

My department's staff never fully understood what I did as part of the executive team, nor did they need to. My participation on the executive team benefited my department if for no other reason than it allowed other executives to personalize the animal health portion of the organization by putting a face to it—my face. And vice versa. Cultivating trusting relationships was then up to us as we worked together for the whole organization.

As I began my education in organizational influence, I quickly realized that I needed to find a better way to lead on all levels—as a leader of my department and as a leader in the organization.

How do we zoo veterinarians gain the kind of influential leadership that fulfills our professional expectations? How do we avoid the traps and obstacles that keep forcing so many of us into the "all-too-common" story?

That was my quandary as I intensified my study of leadership. My answer would come in rethinking the *kind* of leader I wanted to be.

Vision for a Better Way

As I mentioned earlier, I had been taught nothing about leadership in all my years of veterinary schooling. I found out early that I had a lot to learn about leadership itself. By the time I joined the executive team, I'd been reading about leadership for years, attending seminars and conferences, and continuing my education at every opportunity. Finally, around 2008, I learned about the concept of "servant leadership," a term coined by a man named Robert Greenleaf back in the 1970s.

The phrase alone caught my attention. Servant leadership?

It seemed counterintuitive, almost oxymoronic. Why would a leader be a servant? I had grown up thinking that being a servant was something to avoid professionally. As a boss, it made sense to treat people well, but not to be their servant! Wouldn't people take advantage of that? Wouldn't the people that I led see that as a weakness? How could I possibly be effective by serving rather than by being served?

The whole idea flipped the notion of leadership upside down.

Most leadership books offered ways leaders could motivate their employees to do their jobs more effectively. They usually touted slightly different approaches to the two most common types of leadership: authoritarian leadership, in which a leader leads by instilling different degrees of fear, and transactional leadership, in which a leader offers rewards of some kind.

Servant leadership provided a different, "bottom-up" view. It emphasized things such as ethics and empathy, working together, building trust, having an awareness of team members' needs, and working toward a goal of motivation from within.

As I continued exploring what servant leadership might mean for me as an individual leader, I learned that Greenleaf also considered organizations capable of servant leadership, believing that such organizations could change the world.

That sounded very much like the goal of the San Diego Zoo and most modern zoos as well.

I was intrigued.

As I began to contemplate what this unusual concept of leadership might offer for service-focused careers and institutions like my own, I thought back to the most effective zoo leaders I'd known. I realized these leaders personified compassion and objectivity, seeing themselves as stewards of organizational health as well as animal health. Not only did these leaders thrive, so did everyone and everything around them.

I thought of a man who'd started as a bus driver at the San Diego Zoo, became its sole veterinarian for a time, then went on to become a giant in zoo research of infectious diseases and ultimately the director of the Zoo's Center for Reproduction of Endangered Species (now called the San Diego Zoo Institute for Conservation Research). He had more honors and awards than I knew existed. The last, and most precious to him, was the Emil P. Dolensek Award, presented to him by the American Association of Zoo Veterinarians. Behind these achievements was a hardworking, humble, regular kind of guy who valued integrity, respect for people, and trusting relationships. With his character traits and his scientific competency, he had developed extraordinary organizational influence.

I thought of my own boss, the general manager of the San Diego Zoo, who hadn't let me quit for even one day back in 1987. Among his long list of attributes, he had an amazing talent for caring—he cared deeply about the Zoo, the animals, and most importantly, the people. I thought back to his gentle admonitions to me, which held rich lessons on how to treat others.

Both men had developed sophisticated leadership skills I now understood were needed in a zoo setting—and they'd had profound influence on the direction of their organizations and the profession.

Most of all, I thought of one of my veterinary school professors. As students, we all saw Dr. Murray Fowler as larger than life. If anyone could have claimed to be the father of zoological medicine, it would have been him. His influence in zoo animal medicine was immense. He was the first to develop a veterinary school curriculum focused on the training of zoo and wildlife veterinarians. He wrote and edited the first book on the topic, *Zoo and Wild Animal Medicine*, in its eighth edition at the time of this writing. Dr. Fowler was a well-respected master of equine medicine and surgery and toxicology who taught generations of veterinarians. I got to know him at the University of California, Davis on weekly group trips to the Sacramento Zoo. On one of those return trips, I had the most memorable and transformative experience in the most commonplace of situations.

After we had spent a busy afternoon working with zoo animals, he told us we were going to stop at a small farm to see the owner about a domestic horse. The owner insisted on seeing no one but Dr. Fowler. In my mind, there was no need for him to do this. There was an equine ambulatory service at the school that took care of clients like this small farm owner and did a great job.

We went there nonetheless.

The horse had a sore on its lower leg that wasn't healing. This certainly was not an emergency. All of us looked at the horse and its lesion with little interest—all of us except Dr. Fowler. He examined the horse and really listened to the owner's concerns, using the situation as a teaching opportunity for those of us who wished it were a zebra. As I watched, I could tell the owner had a loyalty to my veterinary professor that I had not seen between other clients and veterinarians. The owner showed him a remarkable degree of trust and respect. The longer I watched, the more I knew I wanted to have work relationships like that.

In that simple moment, Dr. Fowler taught me four things I have never forgotten:

1. *We are not as important as we would like to think we are.* He'd figured this out long before I met him. He was important and larger than life to us, but he did not think of himself more highly than anyone else. He was humble and realistic about his ultimate importance in the big scheme of things.

2. *Competence is only part of the equation; character is what sets us apart.* It's important, of course, to be capable and get results. As students, those were the things we were focused on—there was so much hard stuff to learn. In the long run, though, competency just gets us in the door. It is not what sets us apart or makes us successful. It is not what creates a good reputation. Those things come from character: how we treat the ordinary people in our lives.

3. *Simple acts of generosity and compassion lead to great rewards . . . in time.* There is a benefit to treating others well, but the reward for doing so may come way down the road or maybe not at all. That's why it is important to treat others well without actually expecting anything in return.

4. *Everyone matters.* No one is expendable, even those who don't seem to warrant exceptional treatment. Dr. Fowler took time for a person and an animal that day that others would have passed by.

I don't remember a single animal we saw at the zoo that day, but I will always remember the lesson Dr. Fowler taught me about how to treat others. My larger-than-life veterinary school professor was an incredible example of someone who had enormous organizational and personal influence and who'd gained it by seeing himself and his work through a servant's heart.

As I studied servant leadership and remembered my mentors, I had a small epiphany. Servant leadership wasn't a new concept for me. I'd seen this kind of leadership in action. I'd even benefited from it.

In fact, the concept of servant leadership is age-old. In servant leadership, relationships are put before results, humility is placed over pride, trust is built and teamwork is fostered, peers and staff are honored, and new leaders are nurtured. If all of this sounds healthy and life affirming, that's because it is. Just as the humans are healthy, so surely are the organization and the animals.

I decided to give this unusual leadership concept a chance. The results, by the time I retired, far exceeded my expectations. As I contemplated what it did for my own leadership, I instinctively knew it could transform any zoo veterinarian's organizational influence if applied the same way.

The entire dynamic can be distilled into a dozen ideas, which you'll find explored at length in the following chapters. The chapters describe these simple, effective principles, incorporating interviews and stories from a broad range of zoological professionals—including curators, veterinarians, animal health professionals, animal care staff, keepers, and executives.

Of course, traps and obstacles to becoming influentially successful will always abound. But if veterinarians and other animal care professionals can find a way to overcome these barriers, they will make the most of their value and serve their organizations to a greater degree.

Servant leadership is one way to do that—it's a less-traveled path but well worth exploring.

CHAPTER 2

Have an Attitude of Service

At an American Association of Zoo Veterinarians (AAZV) meeting a few years ago, I was attending a talk being given by a former employee who'd gone on to a leadership position elsewhere. A gifted veterinarian, he had been one of the most resistant to the concept of servant leadership.

On the screen at the front of the room, he'd written the word *ME* in big letters with other job roles written in tiny letters around the periphery.

That made me pause. He'd been one of the best animal care professionals, skill-wise, we had at the Zoo at the time. And he knew it. A veterinarian known for his keen intellect, surgical skills, and specialized zoo experience, he was a textbook case of chapter one's all-too-common story. I recalled thinking about his tremendous potential at San Diego Zoo Global when I'd first met him. But I also recalled worrying about what I perceived as a sense of entitlement based on his successes and superior intellect. That slide on the screen said everything about the attitude he'd had when we first met.

Standing before the packed room, he pointed to the big ME on the screen and said, "That was *before*."

A new slide popped up on the screen. This one had all the other roles in large letters in the middle with a tiny ME along the edge.

"And this," he said, "is *after*."

His talk was all about his transition from being an "individual contributor" to being a "department head"—and the changes in attitude that came with it. When he credited, to a large degree, his time in San Diego as the reason for his change and his current success, I couldn't help but smile.

Upside-Down Leadership

In our modern culture, the word *servant* naturally brings up thoughts of submission, servitude, and loss of freedom and rights. It certainly did for me. I preferred to believe that my achievements were my own and so was the recognition. Who didn't?

So, naturally, when I first mentioned the servant leader approach to my department leaders, some objected to the idea that their job was to be a servant to anyone or anything. Some advised me to "tone it down" to make the concept less objectionable by suggesting phrases like "service-based leadership" or "participative leadership."

I certainly could have used one of those terms for this leadership book. But while such phrases shed light on the idea, they do not communicate the transformative, personal power of the phrase "servant leadership."

The concept of a service-focused career is deeply embodied in the word *servant*. The first dictionary definition of *servant* is "a person who performs duties for others." But the second definition is "steward"—a manager who has considerable influence and power over all things occurring in the household, or in our case, the organization. To my mind, that's the clearest meaning of the term: a servant leader, just like a good steward, has an incredible opportunity to exercise broad organizational influence.

When Robert Greenleaf came up with the concept of servant leadership in the 1970s, he was looking for a better leadership model than the command-and-control model prevalent after World War II. His original essay, called "The Servant as Leader," was based on a story of a group of men on a mythical journey. The group had a servant named Leo who did most of the chores but was also the unspoken leader holding the group and the journey together. When Leo disappeared, the men found themselves leaderless and in chaos. The lesson was that the group of men had given Leo the role of *leader* because of his nature as a *servant*.

That story turns the traditional thinking of power and authority upside down, and it makes sense to me. True leadership is something that's given and can't be taken away. Most of us who have been in leadership positions know that having authority doesn't mean we can make people do whatever we want. Ultimately, employees are like volunteers in that they can choose to do what they want. If we require them to do something against their principles or desires, they can leave. If they stay, the result can be even worse—they can comply with malicious intent or avoid achieving the results that their leader had in mind.

Learning to motivate and engage employees is far more effective than holding them accountable with threats. The more I learned about this upside-down take on true leadership, the more I thought it could motivate employees and lessen the usual leader/employee struggle of wills.

It's Not about Me: Changing Mind-Set

As I evaluated the concept of servant leadership, I came to the conclusion that my department needed to adopt its practices. Our department name was Veterinary Services, after all. We were by definition a service department. Yet we did not behave that way. We had become a bit taken by our own image and importance as veterinary professionals.

When zoo veterinarians first start out, we tend to get carried away with our immense responsibility to animal health, especially during emergencies.

Intense focus is certainly warranted in such circumstances to get the job done. That intensity of focus, however, may skew our thinking. It can lead us to think our function in the organization is the only important one— that we are the ones who need to be served. This results in damaged relationships and loss of influence.

Our department's technical knowledge and skills were needed, to be sure. But I couldn't deny that many of us were blind to the fact that others did not see us as we saw ourselves.

I had already begun to grasp that technical ability is only part of what is needed for success—even in a technical field. What really makes someone successful is the value that person adds to others. So technical ability, regardless of how sophisticated it is, makes a difference only in the context of its value to others. For the zoo veterinarian or animal specialist who is really good at technical work, this can be difficult to hear.

I remember a story about one of our veterinarians at the Safari Park. He had just started working for us and was responding to an emergency concerning an animal giving birth in one of our field enclosures.

Racing to the scene in one of the Safari Park's back-road vehicles, he and a technician were stopped by safety cones blocking the road, which were going to force them to take a detour. A maintenance employee was digging a hole to repair a water leak and had set up the cones as required. The veterinarian, however, chose to ignore the detour. He got out of the truck, moved the cones aside, and drove through. As the maintenance worker protested, the veterinarian leaned out his window, calling back as they sped away, "That's why you dig ditches."

It would have been an ironic justice if they had driven into the ditch, but they arrived safely and dealt with the animal medical emergency. Here, though, is where the story takes a pleasant twist.

On the way back to the hospital, the technician decided to talk to the veterinarian about the incident. She approached the matter respectfully but in a straightforward manner. She explained that it was not the way people treated each other at the Safari Park.

To the veterinarian's credit, her remarks got him thinking. Later that day, he called the maintenance department, learned who the man was and where he was working, and went to apologize. Afterward, the two men grew to like each other, establishing a friendly relationship that lasted for years.

In the heat of the moment, especially when we are rushed and carrying a burden of responsibility, it is easy to justify treating people as obstacles, to believe the situation is more "all about me" than "all about being of service." But this story points out how unnecessary and damaging that behavior is. It also reminds us that when we fall short and react the wrong way under pressure, we can still have some good come from it—just by making a change from an attitude of self-focused authority to an attitude of service.

Modeling Upside-Down Leadership

Now that I was convinced my department needed to adopt a servant leadership attitude, I had to determine how to best convince the team to do so. I finally decided the most practical first step was to model it myself. I had to change first. To do that, I had to work on my leadership mind-set.

I began asking myself questions to translate the theory into practice. Some of the questions were:

- Do I serve myself or others?
- Where is my focus?
- When things go well, who gets the credit?
- Am I willing to be vulnerable and show my weaknesses?
- How and when do I say no?
- Do those I lead grow as people?

- Do those I lead become more independent?
- Could those I lead become servants themselves?

The answers to these questions helped me distinguish an outward, self-less mind-set from an inward, self-serving mind-set. Once I saw the distinction in my own thinking, I began attempting to change my own behavior. Sometimes I felt a change. Other times it felt forced and didn't work at all. I realized that even with the right (or progressively right) mind-set, it often didn't feel natural, especially when it went against my human nature. So I added a new question to my list:

- What is my motivation?

To make serving others a natural response, I had to be brutally honest at all times about what was motivating me. When I was motivated by ego or a desire to advance my own needs first, I did things and said things that damaged relationships. When I tried to understand and care about the other person, I was more likely to have a better outcome.

I had to keep reminding myself, "It is not about me." With that mind-set, my idea of success wouldn't be measured by what I got out of it (i.e., recognition, advancement, position). It would be measured by how well I served the needs of others in order for *them* to be effective in their jobs.

Besides, if they were effective, wouldn't that make *me* a successful leader?

This revelation in my own thinking was the essential first step. But I knew it was important to take this concept beyond just a philosophy.

I discovered the Servant Leadership Institute, a local nonprofit organizational consulting and training company. The institute's founder wanted to teach others how to inspire and equip the people they influence. This institute had developed a useful set of behaviors and practices to follow that were geared toward serving others, such as building trust, having values to live by, listening well, keeping thoughts positive, adding value to others, making tough decisions when needed, and doing what is right regardless of the consequences. When done consistently, these behaviors seemed to offer great potential for building trusting relationships and would encourage others to do the same.

But how was I going to convince my staff of that potential, even assuming I was correct about servant leadership being the answer to our departmental problems?

I could think of only one way.

I had to start sharing what I was learning with *all* my department members to see what they thought.

It's Not about Being Nice

As you might imagine, I got a variety of reactions. Only a few of them were positive. The idea that serving others can increase one's influence is deeply counterintuitive. Still, I hoped most people would come around if I kept discussing and modeling it.

One staff member, though, expressed a troubling concern. This person was a veterinarian whose temperament I thought would be a good match for servant leadership. Yet she said she feared people would take advantage of her. Unless all the teams we worked with were required to behave as servant leaders, some individuals could use it as an opportunity to gain the upper hand. She worried that without a trusting relationship already in existence, offering to serve others' interests over her own would be an invitation for abuse and mistreatment. Being "nice" would backfire.

That is a valid point.

By adopting servant leader behaviors, we do make ourselves vulnerable to those who desire to take advantage. Putting ourselves in a position that seems to rely on the mercy of others would cause anyone fear. But that fear is overblown. It rarely happens that way.

Servant leadership is not about being nice. Neither is it about being overly inclusive in decision-making and failing to establish direction. Having a temperament that avoids conflict at all costs is not what it takes to be a servant leader. Servant leadership is a courageous style of leadership that requires quiet, steady strength and character traits such as responsibility, humility, vulnerability, and wisdom.

It also sometimes requires risk-taking, as does any worthwhile effort for building trusting relationships. That is where courage comes in. People look at us differently when we offer to serve their needs. If we are sincere in our efforts to serve them, they no longer view us as a threat. Power struggles cease to exist. Therefore, the trust level in the relationship grows, which ultimately grows our influence with them and beyond.

I don't think I ever convinced that team member, but I pressed on. I began a yearlong effort to regularly expose my department members to the principles of servant leadership. At each of our department meetings, I would reserve ten to fifteen minutes to cover some aspect of the subject. The reactions I received over time ranged from enthusiastic understanding to skeptical resistance.

By the time the year was over, most people seemed to think it was at least a good idea. But even though the introduction to servant leadership had started to change the way people thought, it had not changed their behavior significantly.

My animal health managers group—the directors and supervisors of the animal health departments at the Zoo and the Safari Park—got together to determine what to do next. We decided to hire an expert in the concept, a professional trainer and facilitator, to work with the departments in an intensive training program to see what would happen.

The Animals Deserve It/You Deserve It

We partnered with an executive coach-trainer through the Servant Leadership Institute. For the next year, he met with both departments for interactive training using the principles of servant leadership and team building. This was the explanation and purpose I gave to our staff at the outset of the training:

A key practice of healthy and productive organizations is investing in the development and growth of its people. In our work, we are constantly focused on fighting extinction and ensuring the health and welfare of animals that we love and enjoy. In order to accomplish that, we must work together with people in an open and constructive manner, working in teams, dealing with problems and conflict, and demonstrating accountability while trying to maintain a healthy work/life balance.

Based on data from our recent surveys, years of struggling to deal with conflict and work/life balance, as well as recent conversations with many of you, we know that we have considerable room to improve as a team. And I know that it starts with the department leaders who are responsible for setting direction.

We have heard you loud and clear and know that we need better tools for working together so that we can become a healthy and high-functioning team. I personally would like to see us become the best, most engaged animal health care team in any zoo anywhere. The animals deserve it. You deserve it.

We held a training workshop for four hours every other month. To be sensitive to the busy schedules of the department members, we minimized the time in class while giving some immediate skills for application on the job. During the six- to eight-week interval between classes, we had regular discussion periods to talk about how we had implemented what we had learned.

We learned, among other things, that we could:

- Use tools for better communication, particularly those tools geared toward resolving conflict
- Look at our training programs and hiring choices differently; we could change the outcome to be one in which teamwork and collaboration were valued as much as individual accomplishments
- Model leadership that served others' needs over our own
- Earn and extend trust with colleagues and work in synergy with them
- Intentionally give up wrestling for control of decision-making in the moment to gain trust, credibility, and influence in the future
- Provide digestible information, clear interpretation, and recommendations to colleagues based on our experience
- Work on improving our own character and integrity, thereby becoming good models of leadership in the workplace

In other words, we learned that ours could be a different workplace, a place where character was valued as much as technical competence and success was measured by the quality of our relationships with people as well as by technical outcomes.

At year's end, we were ready to graduate. As the final workshop approached, our trainer explained that he wanted each group to communicate what it had learned. He asked me, "Who are your organization's key leaders? Who would your staff most want to influence and tell what they learned through all this training?"

I thought of my direct boss, plus our CEO and the rest of the executive team, and told him so.

He said, "I want you to invite them to come for one hour of that final workshop to hear each group's presentation."

I was skeptical—both about my team giving presentations and inviting the executives to hear them. Being animal people, the members of our team were not into theatrics. And our executives, busy with the operation of our big institution, surely wouldn't be interested in hearing the presentations of frontline employees about leadership and communication. But our trainer said that this would be the most important part of the entire effort. Our team members, he explained, needed to internalize these concepts, and our executives needed to see the impact this training had made on our team.

I did get a lot of pushback from our staff. They were busy with life-and-death animal care challenges. Our daily work was serious business, after all. They did what they were asked, though, and I was amazed at what they produced. Their presentations were full of creativity, humor, and substance.

The executives who came to the presentations had a chance to comment after each one, and our team members had the chance to show these key leaders what they had learned. Most surprisingly, the experience changed the way the executives perceived veterinarians and the entire animal health staff. The executives showed a new respect for us, seeing that we no longer wanted to be limited to our special expertise but desired to collaborate with them.

In this one act of sharing our training-inspired aspirations with our executive team, we improved our organizational influence dramatically.

Employee Satisfaction Survey

A few months later, our annual employee satisfaction survey was conducted. For managers like me, the comment section is always difficult to read, since the anonymous nature of the comments frees people to be less respectful than they would be face-to-face. But I was surprised and pleased with the responses we got concerning the yearlong team training. Virtually all the comments were positive. Here's a sampling:

- "We are working to improve personal relations within our department. People are becoming aware of their impact on others. We are all expected to treat each other with respect."
- "Recently, our department managers made an incredible investment in making our department even better by asking us to participate in a team training program. Although some of it was tough to get through, it has made it much easier to communicate and hold ourselves accountable for what we do."
- "I wish servant leadership training was a requirement for all staff and management roles in our organization."
- "The opportunity we had to participate in the team training workshops was phenomenal. It was time and money well spent. What a privilege it was to receive this training; what we learned is beneficial in life as well as in work."
- "The training helped me to understand that others in the department may approach a task differently than I do as well as process information differently. Being aware of the differences helps strengthen the team because instead of judging, we are respecting."

Over the following years, we continually fine-tuned what we'd learned to fit our specific zoological departmental and organizational needs, and the effort resulted in measurable change. I soon noticed an increase in the influence of our department. And it grew from there—starting with an attitude of service.

CHAPTER 3

Be Humble

In 1994, Karen made national news with her life-and-death story. Karen was a two-year-old orangutan with a problem. She did not have a critical bloodline, nor would she be part of the breeding program for orangutans in US zoos. But her story changed me and many others in profound ways.

Karen was not growing as she should. We examined her and discovered a heart murmur.

We enlisted cardiologists from the community to help us figure out what was going on. It turned out that she had an atrial septal defect, or ASD, a congenital defect in between the two upper chambers of her heart. Left untreated, she would likely develop heart failure and not survive long into adulthood.

The repair would require open-heart surgery and heart-lung bypass. The procedure had never been performed on a great ape. That, however, didn't stop specialists in the medical community from offering their skills to give Karen a full life. With the aid of a team from the University of California, San Diego (UCSD) medical school, we prepared to perform an unprecedented open-heart surgery on Karen.

We re-created the UCSD cardiac operating room in our operating room at the San Diego Zoo. This took months of preparation and coordination. The surgery began early one Saturday morning in late August 1994. Dr. Stuart Jamieson and his team performed the surgery with perfection. The patch filling the defect worked just as planned. The UCSD anesthesia team's work was flawless. The heart-lung bypass team kept Karen's body alive while her heart was stopped and opened for surgery.

The surgery seemed to be a great success, and the recovery looked straightforward, so the surgery team went back to UCSD to perform a heart transplant on a little girl that very afternoon. By noon, things were getting back to normal around our hospital at the Zoo. A few of us stayed late in the afternoon, and Karen's keeper, Mike, was assigned to watch her. Karen was in an oxygen-rich environment, and we kept an eye on her oxygen saturation. Around five o'clock that afternoon, though, I could see she was getting agitated and her oxygen saturation was trending downward. Mike, who was planning to spend the night with her, was the only other person there. As I considered what to do, Karen's oxygen saturation dropped precipitously. She was in danger of dying if I didn't do something immediately. I decided I had to re-intubate her. Her keeper was excellent, but he did not have experience holding an animal to be intubated, so the two of us struggled with the nearly unconscious animal with just seconds left to save her.

I have heard that in extremely stressful situations, the fight-or-flight reaction takes over and so much blood is diverted to our muscles that we "gray out." That's exactly what happened to me—I "grayed out." I could see only shades of gray and a little color. So much was going through my head in those few moments. I tried to focus on the task at hand, but I was overcome with thoughts of Karen's life, the investment we had just put into this major procedure, and all the people who cared about this animal. All of that was at risk in those moments. And it was in my hands.

But then . . . the tube went in. We began ventilating her manually with a bag. Her oxygen saturation quickly came back to normal, and she became responsive again. Mike and I were both pretty shook up, but as he kept manually ventilating her, I started making phone calls. The anesthesia crew from UCSD returned to the Zoo hospital to aid us in managing her overnight. They had not planned on this kind of commitment, but I was relying on them—probably with a desperate expression—to help us. After some discussion, they called one of their anesthesia fellows who'd also completed the neonatology fellowship. They described him as someone with crazy optimism who never gave up, which was what we needed. He came in that very morning and led the effort to bring Karen around.

Day and night for the next week, we kept breathing for her, hoping time would heal her lungs. And the most amazing thing happened. The medical community in San Diego came together to help us care for her. Doctors, nurses, respiratory therapists, and other medical professionals volunteered their time and expertise to care for Karen. Our own veterinary staff split their time between twenty-four-hour care of Karen and their regular duties.

After one week, we attempted to remove the breathing tube, but Karen was still not able to breathe on her own. That was a Saturday.

The next morning, I was with Karen and a physician who had volunteered to come in for the UCSD anesthesiologist, who had made sure we would have help when he couldn't be there.

What I first remember about the fill-in anesthesiologist was his demeanor. It was Sunday, and he acted as if he were at home relaxing. In fact, he had brought the Sunday paper, and he soon settled in a comfortable chair, perusing it. I, on the other hand, was all nerve endings after the long hours. Here we were a week into intensive care, and Karen still was not able to breathe on her own. I couldn't help thinking about the meeting I'd scheduled for the next morning with all the people who had a stake in the outcome: our CEO, the mammal and primate curators, the director of public relations, our entire veterinary staff, and the volunteer UCSD anesthesiologist. I needed a plan for that meeting, which I was intending to lead. But as I sat there with Karen, I could only come up with questions that I needed to answer myself:

- How long will this go on?
- If we decide to continue this level of care indefinitely, will we be able to muster enough help from the medical community, or will we be on our own?
- After all this investment in Karen and her care, is it even possible to call it quits?
- Will our own veterinary staff be able to continue handling the double duty of monitoring Karen and taking care of the rest of the Zoo's animals?
- With all this focus on one animal, how many other animals are missing out on needed attention?
- What are we falling behind on that will cause problems later?

I watched the fill-in volunteer physician reading the paper, so calm in the face of our mounting tension, and I was almost put off. Instead, I heard myself admitting all my concerns to him. With Karen on a ventilator next to us, our conversation turned profound.

After he listened to all my worries, this kind and wise physician put down his paper, looked at me over his reading glasses, and said, "You need commitments. You need to firm up these relationships you're depending on. At your meeting on Monday morning, after you discuss the details of Karen's condition and hear the points of view of the stakeholders, ask each of them to answer this question: 'Are you and your team willing to commit yourselves and your resources until we resolve this case one way or another?' Make sure you get an answer from each person."

I understood immediately the significance of what he was saying.

The next morning, I met with the stakeholders as planned. We all heard each other out. You could sense the tension in the room when we realized that we had to make a decision. When I asked the question that my physician friend had suggested, I made eye contact with each person. I was honestly surprised to hear each team leader commit to do whatever it took to continue with Karen as long as was necessary. A sense of resolve and relief—and new energy—filled the room as we made plans for the rest of the week and our next extubation attempt. We also made plans to mitigate the negative effects that putting these resources toward one animal was having on the rest of the collection.

Karen's story includes examples of so many of the principles discussed in this book—unity through diversity, connecting with purpose, having an attitude of service. But for me, this part of the story was a perfect example of the power of humility. By allowing myself to be vulnerable to a man I'd just met, I got the very answer I needed to help all those involved—and I received a valuable lesson in leadership.

Humility Is Power under Control

True humility involves having authority but choosing not to use it. This, surprisingly, adds to one's authority. Humble leaders acknowledge others' free will and persuade and influence rather than coerce. I experienced a remarkable example of this immediately after our experience with Karen.

After two weeks in intensive care, Karen finally recovered. The team, however, was worn out. We were all happy about the miraculous outcome, but those of us who had worked most closely with Karen were a tad resentful of the long hours we had put in. Our colleagues who had carried the burden of continuing day-to-day operations without a full staff were a tad resentful as well. Yes, something wonderful had been accomplished that made national news and fostered new partners in the fight for animal welfare, but our sense of teamwork had been threatened, and the value of a successful outcome was on the verge of being lost.

About that time, our CEO called me into his office to express his appreciation. Of course, I was pleased our team had rallied for this cause and partnered so well with everyone involved. It was my CEO, however, who helped me understand the opportunity of the moment. He suggested that we bring the entire veterinary staff to his office—those who had worked on Karen and those who had not.

So we did. As we crowded into our CEO's office, he thanked us all for our role in the success we had achieved for the organization and for this individual orangutan—and he subtly thanked me for my leadership. That expression of thanks from the top of the organization directly to the entire staff was much more effective than if I had come from his executive office to offer his thanks secondhand.

It led to a sustained boost to everyone's morale. We all came out of that meeting invigorated and feeling more like a team than ever before. The CEO's gesture highlighted an important characteristic of humility: it is important for leaders to acknowledge the accomplishments of their teams rather than take credit for themselves. But there is a greater lesson in humility here that could easily be missed, and it involved a position of power. Our CEO displayed true humility—twice. He acknowledged my team's contributions, but at the same time, he honored me in front of my staff. He lifted me up *and* lifted them up, and no one really noticed that he orchestrated it all, not wanting to divert the attention he intended only for us. That is "power under control." Later, when I reflected on what he had done, I made a point to remember and to learn from it.

The concept of power under control also makes me think of a governmental veterinary medical officer (VMO) I came to trust. When I was responsible for animal health at San Diego Zoo Global, I found myself working with government agencies during two separate foreign animal disease threats that could have turned into crises. During any disease crisis, the state has the power to close a zoo and even depopulate its animals if the facility is deemed a threat to the domestic livestock industry. This VMO prepared us during these threats so that we could avoid being a risk to the state's agriculture industry and protect our animals at the same time if our facilities were affected. Although we knew she had the power and the authority of the state of California, we were confident she would avoid using that power if possible, because she had gotten to know us and our operation. This was a welcome service that allowed us to be more prepared than most facilities for foreign animal disease threats.

Then she went a step further. She brought in colleagues who would be influential in the government's decision-making process during an actual outbreak to make sure they understood how prepared we were. She wanted to develop a strong relationship with us as well as make sure she did her job of protecting the state's agriculture industry. She was humble about her position of power and used that power for selfless purposes. By the time I retired, she was highly influential with us. We trusted her motives to the point that we were eager to hear any suggestion she made that might help us be better prepared for the next crisis.

These two stories show that being humble is not a sign of weakness; indeed, humility requires a good deal of strength and assertiveness. Humble leaders have self-confidence but do not project an attitude of self-importance. Humility is an honest approach to reality; it is an acknowledgment that we are not more important than other people. With motivation and practice and a fair bit of introspection, anyone can be an authentic and humble leader.

Yet just as we don't react positively to the word *servant* in the context of leadership, we don't usually associate the word *humble* with great leadership and influence building. Winston Churchill quipped that a political rival was "a modest man who has much to be modest about." That is how many of us see humility: as a weakness we do not want to show. A humble leader, however, has strength and power.

Humility is power under control. And it is essential.

Humility Is Sharing Credit for Successes

So often in zoo veterinary medicine we neglect to celebrate our successes. There's good reason for this. Once an animal gets better, we as zoo veterinarians are done with our job. Besides that, other animals need our attention.

But after Karen recovered and our CEO thanked us for our dedication to Karen's care, we decided it was important to take a break and celebrate among ourselves the miracle of what had happened.

One evening a month or so after Karen had recovered and gone back to her habitat, we invited everyone who had participated in her procedure and extended care to a celebration. Several dozen people arrived, and we gathered first in front of her enclosure. Karen's keeper brought her out so that everyone could see how well she was doing. The keeper wore a T-shirt that said, "We opened our hearts for Karen." It was a clever play on words that our CEO had suggested.

The evening progressed to a banquet and a ceremony where we passed out certificates of appreciation and everyone got a T-shirt. Most of all, we acknowledged the broad support from those who had made Karen's recovery possible. There were no egos there that night. Everyone was gracious about sharing the credit.

Humility Is Attractive

Zoo veterinarians, in general, have passion and resolve. Partnered with humility, that passion is powerful. But without the type of humility that deflects attention and gives credit to others, such intense resolve can be intimidating and objectionable.

Those who act humbly can counter this tendency and be welcomed as leaders. When I say "act," I don't mean to role-play, even though choosing to behave in a humble manner may be a first step. Leaders can be taught behaviors that make them *look* humble, but humility is more effective and real when it is connected to character. Authentic humility is more about who we are rather than how we act. It is a leadership attribute that can be developed. It just requires a high degree of self-awareness and empathy.

Truly humble leaders are attractive. By this I mean they are likeable. They attract loyalty and support. We trust them. Humble leaders put others at ease, developing lasting relationships with the people they influence. We want to be associated with them, and we gladly acknowledge their authority.

Humility Is Seeing the Big Picture

Zoo veterinarians who wish to play an influential role in their organization will find, surprisingly, that humility is an asset on the executive level. They may think their role is to speak for the animals and to represent their departments at the executive level, and it is. But as my zoo leader interviews revealed, executive committee members welcome those who can step away from their singular focus as veterinarians and see the big picture.

A few years after I started on the Zoo's executive team, I received an unexpected gift that taught me something new about humility. It came from an unlikely source—our organization's new strategic plan, Lynx 2.0, which was implemented in 2008. Since I was one of the few "animal peo-ple" on the executive team, I naturally assumed that I would have some responsibility for the animal- and conservation-related implementation teams. You can imagine my surprise, then, when I was assigned to be the leader of the Experience Team. What was that? It was a team whose primary goal was "to enhance the guest facilities and maximize revenue." The overall objective of this implementation team was "to ensure that we preserve and sustain our world-class facilities and guest experience."

I kept thinking, wouldn't I be more valuable on an "animal" team? When I pointed this out to the person in charge of the implementation, I learned that my assignment had come from the top. It had been our CEO's idea. He was looking for ways to break down departmental barriers and eliminate the silo effect so common between the animal people and the operations people. That sounded like a great idea, but I still thought my expertise would be better suited for something related to animals.

After learning about the CEO's decision, I happened to bump into him. With a laugh, I said something to the effect, "Do you *really* want me to lead the Experience Team?"

His cheerful answer: "Yes, I do."

Sensing (and hoping) he knew something I didn't, I decided to trust him and do my best, my discomfort notwithstanding. I remember trying to call together the first meeting of the Experience Team. I didn't even know who most of the people assigned to the team were. We had several tasks we were supposed to concentrate on, none of which I knew a thing about. There were topics like pricing, funding opportunities, internal and external markets, and facility design. I learned that we had experts on staff for each of these topics. And here I was, the director of veterinary services, leading— or should I say, attempting to lead—the entire team.

I had a steep learning curve that year.

I learned that animal health is not the only important department in a zoo. I learned that even though my team members respected me in general,

I had to earn their trust as a leader before they would follow my lead. Most of all, I learned a lesson in humility by serving the organization as a whole, rather than just serving myself or my area of special interest.

I think that's what my CEO wanted—for me to step away from my singular focus as a veterinarian to see the big picture. The year ended with our group completing the tasks we were assigned, and we were all pleased with the team's results. In addition to getting a lesson in humility, I also developed new working relationships with colleagues I otherwise would never have gotten to know. That serendipitously helped to broaden my department's organizational influence. (Even so, at the end of the year, you can imagine how glad I was to get back to my animal health comfort zone!)

It takes a good grasp of humility to change focus, listen, learn, and serve the whole organization. Those who do will almost assuredly find themselves, as I did, in a strong position of influence that benefits their animal focus as well.

Leading with humility allows us to be authentic. It shows strength of character, not weakness. When we think about those leaders who influenced us most, chances are they were humble in some deep, essential way.

Put Relationships before Results

A few years after that day in 1987 when I'd quit only to start over as the San Diego Zoo's director of veterinary services, everything finally had jelled. Building a department from the ground up while keeping up with the demands of a busy zoo practice had been a struggle. Each bit of progress had taken far more time than I'd thought. But I recall the moment that everything felt right. The four veterinarians on our team all shared the same values and had vastly different but complementary strengths. Our expanded technical staff had lightened our veterinary load in dramatic ways. Our managers were energetic and creative and had created a collegial work environment. Our relationships with the animal care staff, curators, pathologists, and others were strong and growing.

Then one day the veterinarian I viewed as my second in command, a young man in his late thirties, began having discomfort in his chest. He was diagnosed with non-Hodgkin's lymphoma. It was treatable if managed early and aggressively, but with variable outcomes. The entire department rallied around him. He kept a brave demeanor, and his courageous attitude brought the entire department that much closer together.

I knew him well enough to know he was worried, though, as anyone would be. He was a son, a husband, and a father. He had a family with two young children. It wasn't hard to guess what he was thinking: What will happen to my children's future if I don't survive? Will I be able to work during the chemotherapy and radiation therapy? Could I lose my job?

Being so young myself, I'd never experienced this situation with an employee. I wasn't sure how to handle it. There were many people I could seek out for advice, but ultimately, it was up to me as the department head to decide what was best for the department.

In addition to my personal worries for my friend and colleague, I had leadership worries. I knew there would be times during treatment that he wouldn't be allowed around animals because of his weakened immune system. I also knew there would be times when he would be too weak to work.

Our animal care work had to be done quickly and efficiently, and it was up to me to get the optimal results from my staff to keep the entire operation running smoothly. If I was only making my decision based on desired results, I would have advised him to take time off on disability and come back when, and if, he got well.

Something inside me, however, knew that my job was about more than just getting short-term results. This person was an asset to me and to the organization. He was a key part of why everything had recently jelled in our department. I realized I needed to keep as much of *that* desired result intact as I could.

He and I discussed realistically what would happen over the next months. There would be times when he could work normally as a clinician. There would also be times when he would have to rest. But we agreed that he would be on-site as much as he could.

His coworkers agreed to cover for him when he couldn't be there, but I needed to find him work that could fit around all these issues. I knew we had several projects that required not only concentrated and uninterrupted time, but also someone with his expertise, strengths, and abilities. So instead of putting him on disability and hoping he'd one day return, I made this a golden opportunity to get that work done.

Of course, his treatment was brutal, worse than anyone expected, and his long-term prognosis was unknown. Through it all, the department members continued to support him. We hoped for the best but secretly prepared for the worst.

Fortunately, the aggressive treatment quickly shrank the tumors, and he went into remission. To everyone's joy, he returned to work and the department returned to normal. But for the next several years, we all worried for him, knowing the cancer could come back.

Five years later, I was coming home from a weeklong backpacking trip in the Sierras with my son and his Boy Scout troop. When we stopped for pizza, I made a phone call to my friend. I knew he'd just had his long-awaited follow-up. If there were no signs of cancer, his oncologist was going to say he was cured. When he answered the phone, I could tell by his voice that it was good news. That was nearly twenty-five years ago. He continues to be cancer free. His children are grown, he is still happily married, and he continues to be a tremendous value to San Diego Zoo Global and one of my best friends.

As a young boss learning as much as I could about leadership, I could have easily made the "correct" decision based on seemingly obvious desired results. Instead, I learned firsthand a valuable lesson: focus first on the people, and the results will follow.

In a Crisis, Focus First on the People

Sudden medical emergencies are a reality in the life of any zoo veterinarian. These high-pressure, high-stakes situations can be emotional for the entire team. At San Diego Zoo Global, the organization's leaders are often present at such scenes. Their purpose is not to direct or judge the actions of the animal care teams but to communicate that the teams are not alone in a high-pressure situation. The leaders are present to care for the needs of the people involved. The attention and support shown by leadership ensures that the animal care teams achieve the best result possible. This philosophy has played out in many crisis situations and has become an unspoken rule: in a crisis, focus first on the people.

I started as an associate veterinarian at the Safari Park in 1982 shortly after a new general manager had arrived. I was occasionally the only veterinarian on duty when my boss was on vacation. One of those times, about a year after I had been hired, two of our twelve African elephants became seriously ill. One had diarrhea but recovered quickly. The second one, Mandavu, did not have diarrhea but became increasingly sick over the next few days. She was reluctant to move. Her blood work indicated an overwhelming systemic infection.

We suspected salmonellosis, a bacterial disease that originates in the intestines and can be life-threatening. While we waited for culture results, we started systemic antibiotics and encouraged her to drink electrolyte water, which she was reluctant to do. By day three, Mandavu was critical, refusing to move. We knew this was serious. We could lose her. Acute salmonellosis requires the administration of large volumes of replacement fluids to rehydrate the animal. In those days, there were few options for providing large volumes of fluids intravenously to large animals like horses, much less an elephant. We did the best we could using multiple intravenous catheters and providing fluids from a series of fifteen-gallon containers perched on the roof.

The lead keeper was passionate about his elephants, particularly Mandavu. She had broken her leg a few years before and had recovered after receiving sophisticated medical care from our veterinary team and nursing care from his team. He closely followed the course of treatment I prescribed, which included putting himself in considerable personal danger. Despite our best efforts, about eleven o'clock in the evening on the fourth day, she collapsed and died in front of us.

Shocked, we were all in despair over her sudden illness and death. The elephant team members were distraught over the loss of one of their animals. I was particularly upset because even though we had the opportunity to respond quickly and aggressively, we weren't able to save Mandavu.

Unexpectedly, our young general manager (who later became the organization's CEO) helped us keep perspective. Despite the late hour, he had come to be with us. He wanted to make sure we had what we needed, but it was his presence and unspoken words that made the difference. That simple act of being with us helped us feel that we were doing the right thing for the animal and the organization, whatever the outcome. The effect was more than a temporary morale boost. It validated the significance of our work. Over the years, he did the same thing, modeling his care of people for other organization leaders. And the results for all concerned were always striking.

In 2011 and 2012, after the Conrad Prebys Elephant Care Center at the Zoo made it possible for us to specialize in the care of geriatric elephants, a series of elephants became seriously ill or died for various reasons. (This would be expected in a facility dedicated to caring for animals at the end of their lives.) Perhaps the most dramatic and difficult case was that of Cha Cha. She was a forty-three-year-old Asian elephant who developed an esophageal obstruction on Christmas Eve. This became a critical emergency, requiring our veterinary and elephant care teams to mobilize immediately for full anesthesia just when everyone was planning to be with their families for the holiday. Furthermore, staff from all over the Zoo—including zoo welders tasked with fabricating special tools—had to rally as well.

Honoring the practice established years ago, the Zoo director and several members of the executive team were quietly present. The animal care workers paid little attention to them as they worked to save Cha Cha, but they knew they were being supported as they cared for the elderly animal. The procedure was tricky and only partially successful in removing the foreign material, and Cha Cha had to be euthanized four days later. The postmortem examination revealed there was irreversible inflammation and necrosis of the lining of the wall of the esophagus, suggesting an underlying disease. While such deaths are challenging for every animal lover, we knew the effort was still worth the personal cost, in part because of the support our leaders showed by being there with us.

The principle is just as important in daily work as it is during a crisis. Good leaders need to demonstrate to their team members that their well-being is a higher priority than the situation at hand. Such leaders remember that while situations are temporary, relationships are long-term. When I forget that—and I have—my default response kicks in. If I have faced a similar problem before or need to reassure myself that I know the problem's solution, I jump in to solve the problem quickly myself. If I focus on the people instead of the problem, though, the team members rise up and resolve the situation themselves.

Another one of my San Diego colleagues demonstrated how this principle can help the people caring for the animals. He oversaw the veterinary care for the Zoo's Hawaii Endangered Bird Conservation Program and was required to manage a very difficult case that he felt would likely fail in the end. That year the team had hatched a large group of Hawaiian crows ('alalā), a highly endangered species, and everyone was excited. But one of the hatchlings was either kicked or fell out of the nest and had a broken leg. The fracture was simple and would have been easy to repair, but the radiographs showed that the bones were lacking adequate mineralization, which was what had caused the fracture. My colleague was forced to advise the managers that the fracture could not be repaired. The bone was not strong enough. The team members kept the bird going, though, treating the soft bone problem with calcium and vitamin D3 so that they could eventually try a repair.

Ultimately, however, the bird developed deformities of the bones. The attending veterinarians realized it would be best to euthanize the bird, which by then had become a beloved animal. My colleague was involved in the discussion remotely. Because he knew the importance of focusing on the people, he advised the veterinarians to bring the entire staff together to talk through the decision. Understandably, there was significant resistance to euthanizing the bird. The veterinarians listened to the staff members' concerns and discussed the situation until the team eventually understood and agreed that euthanizing the bird was the only humane option.

My colleague allowed the situation to take its course, supporting those involved as they reached the best conclusion for the injured bird. He also mentored his staff members along the way to ensure that they paid attention to the needs of the people first. Because of that, the endangered bird team and the younger veterinarians trusted him, and his level of influence became exceedingly strong.

Paying attention first to relationships is a fundamental part of serving others and gaining organizational influence. Any leader who does this creates a solid foundation for trusting relationships, and collective goals and results almost always follow.

Not Avoiding Responsibility

Putting people before results, however, does not mean avoiding responsibility. I've heard that criticism more than once. It seems valid. After all, couldn't putting people first and showing compassion in the workplace validate poor performance?

Done poorly, that is exactly what happens.

In fact, I have been guilty of this myself. I remember a situation in which one of my employees was having a damaging influence in the workplace. For months, I was the empathetic boss. I thought that by modeling empathy and giving the person the opportunity to change, I was doing a good job. The person's behavior got worse, though, and the morale of the entire department suffered. My misguided compassion prevented me from challenging the employee to improve. I was avoiding the hard work of providing clear expectations and holding that person accountable.

Eventually, I did hold the person accountable, the employee decided to retire, and the overall health of the entire team immediately improved. Putting relationships first may be demanding work requiring extra thought and care, but it does not mean leaders tolerate talented people performing poorly.

Putting people before results does require additional skills, to be sure. To make this leadership concept work, a leader must be able to hold people accountable, set goals, and make good hiring choices. A leader must also be willing to terminate employment if nothing else works.

These skills, used in the right way with empathy and compassion, fill the vast majority of people with energy and courage. Employees and teams see someone in their corner, willing to challenge them to be their best.

In short, putting relationships before results bolsters team trust, influence, and ultimately the health of the entire organization. When we place results before people instead, we run the risk of depriving our organizations of the human element, which is critical in making the right things happen.

Measure of Success

Well, then, how does a servant leader measure success? Traditional measures such as financial outcomes are obviously still important. That should be expected. But if we are focusing on people first, we will want to know if we are being successful in that area as well. That brings me back to Robert Greenleaf. He said the test is whether the person we serve is better off because of us. We should ask ourselves, are those we serve growing as people? Are they becoming healthier, wiser, freer, more autonomous, and more likely to become servants themselves?

This is a terrific way of looking at success. It requires that we focus our efforts on others and not ourselves. It demonstrates that we succeed best when those we influence succeed. The practice of servant leadership has the power to transform both the leader and the one served. And the end result is having trusting and respectful relationships that flourish.

CHAPTER 5

Build Trust

I was on the phone with the animal care manager in charge of the Children's Zoo. I was beside myself. We were discussing whether to put a young gazelle on intravenous fluids overnight in the nursery. Even though doing so would require more resources, the treatment was clearly indicated for the animal's well-being. The manager was not going along with the plan, though. He seemed suspicious.

I finally said, "Don't you trust me?"

The pause that followed told me he did not. He had no reason to trust me or to have confidence in what I was recommending. We had not worked together for very long, so he didn't know me well enough to judge my character or to believe what I was saying. He couldn't evaluate my abilities either, because he had not seen the results of my previous clinical decisions.

I had to work hard to explain why this was a good decision and worth the extra resources. In the end, he extended trust to me, and the animal got its fluids. The moment reminded me how important it is to have vital, trusting relationships with our coworkers: these relationships will provide the most successful outcomes for the animals under our care.

The Line of Trust

Trust is among the most fundamental qualities of human relationships, the glue that holds teams of people together.

We depend on trust to protect and sustain relationships. Trust means that we believe in another person's reliability. Almost every interaction with another living being, human or animal, involves trust. Either the trust is high or it's low.

We all can think of at least one person with whom we have a high trust relationship. That relationship feels special. Communication is quick and easy. Work is enjoyable. Things get done with little effort. Confidence is sky-high. Such relationships produce exceptional financial and mission-related results.

The opposite is true with a low-trust relationship. Confidence is low, and suspicion is sky-high. Mahatma Gandhi said it this way: "The moment there is suspicion about a person's motives, everything he does becomes tainted."

Trust engenders confidence, and lack of trust leads to suspicion. A continuum exists between these two states. But a clearly defined line of trust separates them, yielding distinct outcomes. When we are in a relationship on the confidence side of the line, communication flows and we assume the best. When a conflict arises, we have faith that we can resolve it. If the relationship is on the suspicion side of the line, though, nothing is easy and every action or motive is doubted. Everything becomes an issue, and we lose confidence that we can resolve a conflict. Our relationships can slip to either side of the line based on our choices and actions. By continually paying into people's trust accounts, however, we can maintain a high level of trust with them.

In my job as a veterinary department head, I always worked hard to develop solid and trusting relationships with the curators. One of the curators in particular worked just as hard to do the same, taking the initiative to build a trusting relationship between us. He took the time to get to know me, invited me for lunch, and offered his help to solve mutual concerns. When our bird collection was threatened with the highly contagious Exotic Newcastle Disease in 2003, he partnered with me to put an ambitious plan in place. Doing so created difficulties for him and his staff, but he understood the necessity and trusted my assessment of the risk. Over the years, we had plenty of opportunities to test our relationship, but because of our level of trust, we gave each other the benefit of the doubt. Although there were many times that conflict could have developed between us, it didn't. The existing trust we'd built up got us through the challenges every time.

Trust Accounts

When I think about trust in the context of the zoo world, I cannot help but think about the ongoing trust that's needed between animals and humans for everything to run in a smooth and healthy manner. That trust is a daily essential, and it can still impress me after all my years working with zoos.

Animal behaviorists and trainers understand and use this concept of "trust accounts" all the time. Trainers especially understand the importance of building trust, because sooner or later something will happen to test that trust, using up some of the accumulated trust.

When I was first starting as a veterinarian, I hated how we had to anesthetize great apes by shooting them with a dart pistol. Great apes are intelligent beings, so when I came into the bedrooms carrying a dart pistol, they knew what was going to happen. Anticipating the hits with the dart, they'd scream and throw objects at me. Not only was it unpleasant for all concerned, physiologically, it was undesirable for an animal to become excited prior to anesthesia. One time I had to dart an orangutan who had never seen a veterinarian with any kind of darting device. A couple of days before the scheduled exam, I approached her with a blowpipe to see her response.

I just lifted the pipe up to my face and pointed it at her. Immediately, she covered her face. I felt horrible knowing I still had to dart her.

Fortunately, the animal trainers found a better way. No one could train great apes to gladly accept being darted, but the trainers could teach them to accept a hand injection of an anesthetic. This gets back to the point of trust accounts. The animals willingly accepted an injection through operant conditioning, a training technique that rewards animals for performing a desired behavior. In essence, the animals are given the choice to perform a certain behavior and therefore are in control of the outcome. No punishment is ever given. It is a better way for all.

Thankfully, I no longer had to dart great apes. Instead of walking into the bedrooms and creating a chaotic and fearful scene, I waited in the truck outside for a calm voice on the radio to say, "Injection given." Positive reinforcement training allowed the great apes to accept the injections willingly, enabling them to remain calm and relaxed prior to anesthesia. But there could be no such reliable training if the team had not developed full and healthy trust accounts with the animals.

Malcolm and the Tiger

Stories of trust between people and animals are particularly appealing and endearing. The following story is also about trust between people and animals, although I doubt you'll find it endearing. This legendary story is one I normally would not have been told. The keepers didn't want anyone to know about it. No one was proud of the incident. I had to earn their trust before they would tell me—and that was no easy accomplishment.

I was in my first year of internship/residency at the San Diego Zoo. Although there was dysfunction in the veterinary and technician groups, the three keepers who worked at the hospital were real professionals. As was true of most of the keepers at the time, these men were on their second career, having retired from the navy. These keepers had seen everything and had figured out, mostly on their own, how to handle any animal. In those days, the term *animal welfare* wasn't yet being used, but they knew how to give the animals the best life possible while under their care. I knew I could learn a lot from these men.

As nice as they were to me, I also knew I would have to earn their trust before they would share much. Since the intern/resident changed every couple years, these keepers put each new person through a series of character tests. In the kitchen was a series of bins filled with fruit. The bin of oranges contained a plastic orange that always looked like the tastiest one. Because interns/residents were always too busy to eat, the keepers knew we would grab some fruit from the bins. I consistently grabbed the "intern orange." I failed the gullibility test, but I must have passed the character test because I laughed with them every time I fell for it.

I thought the best way to earn the keepers' trust would be to have lunch with them, but they were hard to find at lunchtime. I discovered that they had created a little haven for themselves underneath one of the hospital holding buildings that was set up with easy chairs, a little carpet to cover the dirt, reading material, and a great view of the eucalyptus woodlands surrounding the hospital. That haven was a secret place where they could escape the never-ending questions of the veterinarians. When I found myself having lunch with them in their special place, I knew I had earned their trust. It was only then that I heard the story.

One of the hospital keepers was particularly friendly and optimistic. Malcolm, as everyone called him, told me about a unique test of trust that became one of survival.

Malcolm had taken care of a male tiger that was being treated at the hospital. This tiger was not tame. But Malcolm spent every extra moment he could with the animal, giving him attention through the cage wire to gain the tiger's favor and providing him with activities. Both the keeper and the tiger clearly enjoyed the interaction, and as it turned out, they developed a special kind of trust.

When it was time to load the animal in a crate and transfer him to his home in the Zoo, Malcolm was the obvious one to position himself above the crate and lift the door to the crate while encouraging the animal to enter. There was a terrible mix-up, however. Another keeper remotely opened the wrong doors, and Malcolm suddenly found himself in the space with the tiger and nowhere to escape. The only way he could get out was to go across the cage to the front walk-through door, which would take him right past the tiger. Quickly, Malcolm decided to climb along the ceiling wire that was suspended above the tiger—a strategy he later admitted probably just made him a more interesting target. Unbelievably, the tiger simply watched curiously as Malcolm performed his antics and made it safely out the front door.

To me, this story was more than an admission of mistakes told by a lucky survivor. It was a dramatic demonstration of the trust account concept before the phrase was even invented. As I began to think about it more deeply, I realized the story about Malcolm and the tiger included lessons about trust that we can apply to our relationships with people.

- *Trust takes time and consistency.* Building trust takes small acts of kindness and getting to know someone's needs and desires. Trust is built by consistently making and keeping commitments. Malcolm did this as part of his job.
- *Trust grows when we extend it to others.* Although we often think we can't trust someone until they earn our trust, it really works the other way around. We tend to trust those who trust us even when we don't yet deserve it. This kind of trust may have been responsible for changing the tiger's innate response. Malcolm may have survived

this unintended incident in large part due to the trust he extended to the tiger. But Malcolm was not stupid. He would never have tried it again intentionally. That's the difference between smart trust and careless trust.

- *Trust requires good intentions and integrity.* Malcolm sincerely wanted the best for the tiger, and the tiger apparently picked up on Malcolm's good character and intentions. Similarly, we pick up on each other's intentions and motives. If we detect a flaw in character, we become suspicious and hold back trust.
- *Trust makes it possible for the impossible to happen.* Malcolm knew what any tiger is capable of doing, but he was not surprised that this tiger left him alone. Trust in work and family relationships makes it possible to achieve wonderful synergy and unexpected results. Conversely, without trust, virtually nothing good can happen.
- *Trust can protect us from harm.* In fact, a trusting relationship can even turn a foe into a friend. Someone with whom we have a strong, trusting relationship will stand up for us when the unexpected happens. Trust certainly protected Malcolm.

Thirty-five years later, I still remember this story and its lessons, and not because of how awful it could have turned out. I remember because of the character of a man who cared enough to build a trusting relationship with a tiger. And it saved his life.

Earning/Extending Trust

In small animal practices, most veterinarians know that trust is the primary component of a healthy, productive doctor-client-patient relationship. Veterinarians who are viewed by their clients as knowledgeable, empathetic decision-makers are also considered more professional and competent.

Another way to understand how to earn trust is by viewing it as a function of character and competence. Our character is *who* we are. Character includes our integrity, motives, and intentions with people. Our competence is *what* we do. Competence is related to technical ability. It includes our capabilities, skills, results, and track records. By working on both our character and our competence, we can demonstrate our trustworthiness and earn the trust and confidence of others.

Building trust requires that we make and keep commitments. For example, a zoo veterinarian may commit to helping design a new exhibit. By honoring the team commitment and contributing to the process, that veterinarian can demonstrate integrity (character) and capability (competence).

Making a commitment creates hope. Following through on that commitment shows character and, when done consistently, creates trust. But what about extending trust to others? Do other people have to earn our trust or can we extend trust without requiring them to earn it? As Ernest Hemingway once wrote, "The best way to find out if you can trust somebody is to trust them."

Trusting relationships are essential to accomplishing the critical work of zoos as well as aquariums. We depend on many key stakeholder relationships for animal care. We have to be smart about trusting others, but we also have to be willing to do so. No relationship is perfect: everyone betrays trust occasionally, willfully or accidentally. Yet we have to keep striving for high trust relationships. They are extremely satisfying, and only those relationships create the kind of influence that can improve an organization.

Trust Lost/Found: A Critical Moment

Trust can be a tricky thing, however, when you are attempting to earn it in a foreign country. How do you trust a stranger from another culture with something as precious as one of your country's giant pandas? And how do you respond when that stranger errantly betrays that precious trust? Are the rules different for different cultures?

In 1998, I found out.

During the height of our work to help the endangered giant panda, I was part of a multi-institutional effort to partner with Chinese scientists and biologists to better understand the captive population of giant pandas and what was preventing them from being a self-sustaining population. At that time, neonatal mortality was high, survival of cubs to maturity was low, and breeding success of the adult population was poor. Although there was interest in helping the wild population, stabilizing the captive population was almost a prerequisite to that.

Our goal for the Giant Panda Biomedical Survey was simply to evaluate the biology and health of the captive population. Doing so would provide direction for us as we worked to manage the population so that it would become sustainable.

On our first visit, we arrived one winter morning in Chengdu, China, the closest city to the Chengdu Research Base of Giant Panda Breeding. I had been in China only one other time; this was still a novel experience for me.

We traveled in winter so that we could finish our work well before the giant panda breeding season. We had flown all night from Los Angeles with our supplies. It was an overcast and dreary morning in Chengdu. The airport was old and outdated—it looked very institutional. We pulled a dozen crates full of medical equipment from the baggage claim area. I always get nervous going through customs even when I just have my suitcase. But there, in a foreign country with loads of odd equipment that was difficult to explain even without a language barrier, I was beyond nervous. Going through customs went surprisingly well, though, and we were met immediately by a group of smiling Chinese scientists.

One of them, Zhang Wei, a young student working at the Chengdu panda base, would become our interpreter and friend. He was the first to greet us. Seeing we were overburdened with equipment and carts, he took two of them and said with a big smile, "This is the beginning of a great collaboration."

That made me relax a bit. In those days, Chinese scientists were suspicious of Westerners, so we were determined to change their perceptions. After all, our goal was to help the giant panda population in China. To do that, we would need to collaborate and develop trusting relationships. None of us were experts on Chinese culture, so we made sure to follow their lead.

That afternoon the first thing we did was meet in a room designed for drinking tea. We would do this at every place we worked in China. It seemed extremely inefficient to me as we sat uncomfortably waiting for someone to speak while watching an elderly man pour hot water into our freezing teacups. But in Chengdu, even in winter, the rooms were unheated, so I was grateful I could at least put my cold hands around a hot teacup.

I soon learned that the tearoom was a very important place. In the tearoom, we not only talked about our plans, but we also began to develop trusting relationships with the key players. They knew from our reputation that we had the ability (competence) to pull off our plan to examine all their pandas under anesthesia. I sensed that they wanted to assess our character, though. They seemed to be using the moment to go deeper into who we were—to see if we were trustworthy.

We all had a chance to talk, and my job was to explain the anesthesia plan. I had learned that their standard procedure was to use high doses of ketamine alone. From my experience with zoo bears, however, I believed this was not the best method. We had discovered that adding a drug for muscle relaxation provided a much better result. We'd successfully used the combination in our female giant panda in San Diego just a few weeks before. So while sipping tea—which was cold by now—I explained all this to the veterinarians, the director, and the other important figures in the room.

I realized that we had gained their trust when they agreed to use our anesthetic regimen, and I knew that we had a lot at stake to maintain that new trust. I worked closely with the Chinese veterinarians, who were keen to see how my suggestion would work. As I drew up the anesthetic combination, I used my relatively new reading glasses in the dimly lit panda bedrooms to see what I was doing. One of the veterinarians, who was watching closely, noticed that I drew up the wrong amount. I quickly corrected it and went on with the procedure. I was still confident in my anesthetic method. But this time, the animal woke up much more slowly than I was expecting or they were used to.

The Chinese veterinarians, keepers, and biologist who were watching us closely were very gracious, considering that my method did not work as well as I had planned. I realized I'd been prideful in thinking that I could provide a better anesthesia regimen than what they had been using for years.

Afterward, everyone involved—both Americans and Chinese—met to discuss what we had learned as a collaborative team. When my less-than-successful method was brought up, I agreed that their experience with ketamine alone as an anesthetic for giant pandas was probably the better choice. That turned out to be a critical moment. By admitting that we could learn from them, I showed vulnerability. Instead of undermining their trust in our competency, my admission seemed to solidify our mutual trust.

The result?

Over that year and the next two years, we examined sixty-three giant pandas in four Chinese institutions, making biomedical assessments on each. We had no anesthetic complications at all. The initial trust that I was given was based on our reputation—for who we were and what we'd accomplished. Although that trust was tested and a bit damaged due to my error, over time we built an even higher level of trust. Today, I still count many of those Chinese partners as friends as well as colleagues.

Trust is indeed a fundamental quality of human relationships, a function of character and competence. In China, we had to develop trust for anything meaningful to happen. That's true for any endeavor, no matter the culture or the country. Meaningful work gets done only with a solid amount of deep trust.

CHAPTER 6

Prevent and Resolve Conflicts

When I was a freshman pre-veterinary student at Fresno State University, I befriended another pre-vet major who also lived in the dorms. We had both worked in small animal practices in high school and figured we'd own small animal practices someday. He was outgoing and enjoyed being around people. I was more introverted and introspective, but we got along great.

Near the end of that first year, the dean of student services at the University of California, Davis spoke at our pre-vet club meeting about the opportunities in zoo and wildlife veterinary medicine. I was intrigued by the stories he told of veterinarians working with cetaceans in the navy, moose in Alaska, and zoo animals in San Diego. His talk opened my eyes to a world I did not know existed. In that moment, I knew I wanted to be a zoo or wildlife veterinarian.

I was so excited by the talk that I went up to the dean afterward along with my friend. The dean was a kind man who gave me his full attention when it was my turn. I thanked him for his presentation and told him how much of an impact it had made on me. I wanted to say something that would express how sincere I was about becoming the kind of veterinarian he had described, so I told him, "I want to be a veterinarian so much because I like animals more than people."

His congenial smile faded a bit. He looked squarely at me and said, "You have to understand something right now. In veterinary medicine, you must like people as much as you like animals. Otherwise, you will live in conflict and the animals will suffer for it."

As we left, my friend gave me a knowing look. He knew exactly what the dean was saying. Many "animal people" gravitate to this kind of work, thinking they can avoid interacting with people. I was one of them. While I was chagrined at the time, I'm grateful the dean cared sufficiently to correct my thinking when I was still young enough to change. He helped me make an important connection that some find hard to understand: conflict between people who care about animals hurts both the people and the animals they care about. To do well, I needed to learn to deal with people—for the sake of the animals, if for no other reason.

But here's the good news. As people who choose a career because of our love and empathy for animals, we have an advantage without even realizing it: we already know how to love and empathize. What we don't often realize is that those same qualities help make successful human relationships as well.

The executive coach who led my team through servant leadership training also worked with several animal science and husbandry groups. He often heard from people who love animals but have conflict with people. One day, a terrific young manager confided in our coach that he had a small problem.

"I can handle the cows," the young manager said. "It's the people I can't handle."

Our trainer asked him to describe how he "handled" the cows.

The young manager said that his boss had told him never to yell or move fast around the cows to avoid making them anxious—to allow the cows to gently lead themselves. The manager added, "He also said to never use a cattle prod or harm the cows in any way."

Then our trainer asked the man to describe how he worked with his staff.

With people, the manager said, he had to be direct to get anything done, usually using an "I'm the boss and you are the subordinate" attitude.

At that, the trainer told him, "In reality, you don't really 'handle' the cows; you simply guide and support them and give them some gentle direction. You are leading them to do the work they need to do. Cows don't like to be 'handled'—and neither do people."

As you read this, you may have thought of a conflict you have witnessed or are currently experiencing. Think of how your response to that conflict could be affecting the animals under your care. Then compare the way you handle animals to the way you are handling these people.

How could you resolve the conflict?

More importantly, how could you have prevented it in the first place?

Preventing Conflict

When I have a conflict with someone, my default tendency is to become inwardly focused and express my self-serving character. When I'm in that frame of mind, I lose my servant attitude, and the situation becomes all about me. I dwell on the effect the other person's actions are having on me. I think about why I am justified to feel the way I do and how I should take action as a result of being mistreated. I look for allies to confirm my biased point of view. All my other values and priorities tend to become less important. The energy and attention I would otherwise put into the important job of ensuring animal health and welfare instead go to protecting myself. I respond this way unless I deliberately take another path.

This is me at my worst. I do not like it, but I do not think I am alone in this particularly human behavior.

You may have seen coworkers become distracted from their work due to an unresolved conflict. Job performance and effectiveness decline. Safety practices are missed, leading to accidents. Most of us can remain professional enough so that a conflict stays in the background without significantly affecting job performance and animal care, but if it goes on long enough, even the most professional people can lose focus, develop a skewed perspective, and become a liability to the team . . . all because of a conflict that could have been prevented or resolved responsibly.

There are three key ingredients in preventing conflict:

1. A servant leader mind-set
2. Trust
3. Role clarity

The first two you've read about in earlier chapters. The third, role clarity, happens when parties decide together who is responsible for what. All three elements work together to bolster relationships.

When I think of how these factors play out in preventing conflict, I recall our close call with avian influenza. In 2007, the dreaded, highly pathogenic avian influenza (HPAI) was extending its reach from Southeast Asia to Europe and into Africa. It was moving so rapidly that it was likely to reach North America within months. This is a devastating disease for domestic poultry, but this strain of H5N1 also had a human disease risk—with the potential to cause a worldwide pandemic in both birds and humans.

In these types of situations, state and federal agriculture agencies have considerable authority to close facilities and cull exposed birds. Zoos around the world were in turmoil about what to do. We in San Diego also were worried. But because of our experience with Exotic Newcastle Disease a few years before, we were more prepared. The diseases are transmitted in a similar way, so we could expand on protocols we had already written.

The head pathologist for San Diego Zoo Global and director of the Wildlife Disease Laboratories partnered with me to lead a multidisciplinary team to create and implement a comprehensive policy and associated protocols to protect our bird collection, employees, guests, and organization. We talked to each other regularly to make sure we were both clear on who would be responsible for what, since confusion and disputes over roles inevitably lead to unhealthy conflicts and loss of precious time. Together, we led a two-day "tabletop" workshop that included managers from all departments at both the Zoo and the Safari Park. I relied on him for his disease risk knowledge and insight into human behavior. He relied on me to draft the written protocols and lead the weekly contingency planning meetings. There was never conflict between us or competition for recognition. In fact, that year at the employee party, we were given a joint award for our work on avian influenza. As far as I know, that was the only time the award was given jointly. We avoided conflict that could have easily developed because we wanted to serve the organization rather than to advance selfish ambition, we'd already developed a trusting relationship, and we had clear roles that we each respected. (More on role clarity and how to achieve it in chapter nine.)

We expect conflict to be a rare event, especially if we've invested in our relationships with our coworkers. In real life, though, even with the best intentions and the best preventive strategies in place, conflict is part of the human experience. When we do the preventive work up front, however, conflicts are much easier to correct.

Preventing Isn't Avoiding

Before we go on, I need to make a distinction between preventing conflict and avoiding conflict. Preventing conflict is smart because it is proactive. Avoiding conflict is trouble because it evades responsibility.

When I first discovered servant leadership, I wanted to learn all I could about my personal leadership strengths and weaknesses. So I requested a leadership survey from my coworkers. This survey asked them about my leadership skills. The question on which I scored the lowest was "Confronts people with problems as they arise." I admitted to myself that it was my nature to shy away from conflict. I much preferred to encourage people than to confront them with criticism. As leaders, however, if we don't hold our staff accountable for expected performance, we are allowing our standards to drop, which leads to mediocre performance and more conflict.

Resolving Conflict

Now that I am retired, I realize that I spent too much time in my office and not enough time out seeing things for myself. I know this because I have many memories of people coming into my office wanting me to "fix" the behavior of one of their coworkers. I liked talking to people and being available, but in those situations, I always felt trapped. I knew I was hearing a skewed view of a conflict in which I was suddenly becoming entwined. Of course, it was understandable that they would come to me with their problems. I was their boss. I had done the same thing with my own bosses over the years. But in the long run, it's a mistake to have a boss "fix" a problem. (To be clear, I am not referring to conflicts that are illegal, unethical, or threaten safety such as harassment, discrimination, and personal threats. I am referring to the normal conflicts that arise when humans work together.)

At one point in my leadership journey, I welcomed the challenge of trying to resolve conflicts between my employees. I was pretty good at coming up with solutions that seemed logical to me. My solutions didn't help, though. In fact, they often inflamed the situation. By inserting myself into the conflict, I ultimately had to become judge and jury when matters escalated. Then neither party was satisfied, so the conflict remained.

Worse, by trying to resolve the conflict myself, I was taking away the responsibility from my employees. This made them more dependent and gave them less control of their own work environment. And having control in our work life is fundamental to being satisfied and engaged in our work.

I became more confident in preventing and resolving conflict only after pushing myself to learn about these subjects through research, workshops, and ultimately experience. A few tools I uncovered made a big difference.

I'm still no expert on conflict resolution. There are hundreds of books written by those who have dedicated their careers to the subject. I've found the following skills especially useful, however, in resolving conflict among well-intentioned zoo professionals.

Take the Direct Approach

Talking directly with the other party is the logical and important first step to resolving conflict. Yet I learned that most people needed to be reminded to do it. So I made it a rule. When employees came to me with conflicts involving other employees, I reminded them of our rule that their first action should be to approach the other employee directly. I also reminded them not to enlist allies in their cause or gossip about the conflict. To provide support, I offered to facilitate the discussion but not to resolve the conflict for them.

Employees often object to this rule, claiming they are not in a position to discipline another employee. That is a job for the manager, they usually say. And they are quite right. No one should discipline another person without the authority to do so. But conflict between two people is not a disciplinary problem. It's almost always a two-way problem that requires direct, mature dialogue to be resolved.

The other objection employees have is fear of making the conflict worse. And they are quite right again. I remember approaching a coworker early in my career about a problem I was having with him. Our conversation did not go well at all and made matters worse between us. In fact, I shied away from talking to him as soon as the problem arose again. In that case, however, I had no tools to properly direct the conversation. Indeed, when I finally did try again, my solution was to approach him with a list of reasons why he was off base. You can imagine how that went. We ended up involving our boss, who did not appreciate having to solve our dispute. We both lost a bit of influence with him as a result.

If I'd approached him directly armed with the skills detailed below, I might have been able to resolve the conflict between us.

Prepare for Key Conversations

We can all recall having a sudden and unexpected conversation that provoked in us an overemotional response. These types of conversations can get out of control and lead to prolonged conflict. We can prepare for them, however, by learning how to recognize and respond to them in a productive way. If we do, these conversations can become safe and constructive, but only if we respect the other party and their interests. We also must manage our own emotions by making sure we have the facts straight before we interpret what is said.

When you are suddenly confronted with an issue that draws you into an emotional conflict:

- Respect the other party and that person's interests
- Don't act on assumptions or emotions
- Seek evidence before responding

I recall one key conversation that came up suddenly. It was the fall of 1996, shortly after the giant pandas Shi Shi and Bai Yun arrived in San

Diego. One of the panda keepers asked me to talk with our Chinese colleagues, who were concerned about Shi Shi, our elderly male giant panda. We were hosting two Chinese representatives from the Wolong Giant Panda Breeding Center. Our animal care and animal health teams were obliged to allow them full access to the animals and consult with them on details of the pandas' care. Despite some trouble with the language differences, our communications and interactions had been friendly and cordial—at least up to that moment.

Our team arrived at the panda bedrooms, where our keeper was visibly concerned as she glanced toward our guests. Shi Shi was in distress. He was acting odd, as if he had pain in his abdomen. He'd passed a large volume of awful-smelling mucoid stool. This was not the first time he'd done that, but it was more dramatic than before. I knew from my previous experience with giant pandas at the National Zoo—where I'd worked after my internship at the San Diego Zoo—that this was not an unusual occurrence. Our Chinese colleagues had seen it before in Shi Shi. But we could tell they were concerned too.

We had formed a theory about this problem in giant pandas. Most pandas in those days received a diet of bamboo and easily digested foods including milk and other sources of animal protein. The traditional thought was that they needed extra nutrients, particularly protein, that bamboo alone could not provide. But their natural diet did not include anything other than bamboo. So our team theorized that if we eliminated the milk and other sources of protein and increased the amount of bamboo, we could avoid this troublesome condition. With this problem becoming more severe and recurring in Shi Shi, it was time to share our theory with our Chinese partners and change his diet.

As we started to talk with them, I realized this conversation could be a turning point or a flash point. It would be a critical one for the health of the pandas and maybe more so for our relationship with our Chinese colleagues. To gain their approval for a permanent change in diet, we had to approach the subject in the right way.

We proposed the theory and a new diet based on that theory. We explained the rationale and the evidence on which we were basing our theory, and we understood that they would be responsible to their authorities. Acknowledging their role, we showed respect for their position and the consequences if something went wrong. In addition, we controlled our emotions and our enthusiasm for our theory by sticking to the evidence. We focused on the health of the animals—not on winning the argument. In the end, our nutritionist explained our position to them in a way that was easy to grasp. He asked them what animal (besides humans) drinks milk past the infant stage, making the point easily understood using evidence and logic. After a few telephone calls back to China, we had their full support. The pandas no longer received milk, the theory proved right, and the uncomfortable mucus blockage became a rare event.

By approaching the issue unemotionally, basing our position on evidence, and respecting the other party's responsibilities and concerns, we worked through what could have been an undesirable situation for all concerned. And both the humans and the animals benefited, just as we all wanted.

Base Decisions on Evidence, Not Assumptions

Using such skills forces those of us in leadership positions to reflect on how we size up situations to make decisions. In 1970, a Harvard Business School professor who was also an organizational psychologist developed a problem-solving tool called "The Ladder of Inference." Using the image of a ladder, he described the thinking process we go through from observing reality and facts to deciding to act. The bottom rung of the ladder is the observing, the top rung is the decision, and the intermediate rungs of the ladder are the stages we go through or, in some cases, choose to skip.

In our busy lives, we are often pressured to take quick action. Evaluating evidence, especially that which is complex or unclear, requires considerable energy. So we often take shortcuts up the ladder.

For example, based on past experience, I may make assumptions about someone else's motives. As a result, any action I take is not based on data from the real world but my own beliefs. Instead, I should approach the person directly and get accurate information. If I do, that data can change my understanding and conclusions, and ultimately, my actions will be more appropriate. Using the ladder metaphor, then, we should begin at the bottom—where reality resides—instead of starting midway up.

This ladder-rung-skipping scenario plays out daily in our lives. For example, I once complained to my boss about a curator bringing in too many animals at one time. If I had approached the curator directly, I would have found out that the animals were part of a confiscated shipment of animals that needed care for a limited time. Understanding the evidence— instead of jumping up the ladder and making assumptions—would have made all the difference.

This should not be a foreign concept to veterinarians. We were trained to seek a diagnosis prior to initiating treatment. The first step in establishing a diagnosis is to collect data. That data collection starts with asking questions to learn the history. Next we perform a physical examination of the entire animal, not just the area we assume is the problem. Then we collect baseline laboratory and imaging data to complete the picture. If we follow this model, we are less likely to make assumptions and jump to conclusions that are not based on reality.

A favorite quote on this subject comes from famous investor Warren Buffett: "What the human being is best at doing is interpreting all new information so that their prior conclusions remain intact." It is a human tendency to pick information that confirms preexisting beliefs and assumptions. In other words, we tend to focus on a subset of data that agrees with our beliefs but does not necessarily represent reality.

When a conflict arises, if we base decisions about people on evidence instead of assumptions, we can stay grounded in reality. We can determine what part of the ladder we are on when we get the urge to make a decision prematurely. We can test our assumptions, beliefs, and conclusions by working our way up the rungs of the ladder. If we are consistent and deliberate, the ladder concept will help us come across as reasonable individuals who can cut through the emotions and confusion that often accompany conflict. This technique can also be used to challenge someone else's conclusions in a nonthreatening way.

If we are aware how even the most logical among us can jump to conclusions, we can allow reality and evidence to drive our discussions rather than unbridled emotions. Doing so benefits our work relationships, builds our influence, and ultimately protects animal health and welfare.

Take a Balanced Approach

The servant leader, of course, must stand up for what is right. It is entirely possible to advocate for a position without damaging the relationship. Arming yourself and a team member with this empowering conflict-resolution skill begins with a quick self-examination:

- What is my motivation?
- Am I seeking to understand, or am I seeking support for my current position?

Keeping the proper balance between inquiring for understanding and advocating a position is a key skill in conflict resolution. In most discussions with people who have strong opinions, we try to impose our ideas on them. This is not an effective approach, but since it is the default approach of our human nature, we must be alert to avoid it. It is far better to achieve balance. When we first seek to understand and then work to gain support for a position, we are in balance. This is when conflict can be resolved and mutual learning is the result. When these processes are in balance, people can commit to action and agree to resolve conflict.

During our team training in servant leadership, one of the most valuable exercises involved practicing such "inquiry and advocacy" behaviors. Our trainer had all of us come to the workshop prepared with a topic we cared about and were interested in advocating. In groups of three, we took turns understanding/inquiring and persuading/advocating.

To seek understanding, we asked open-ended questions without judgment to those speaking. Open-ended questions encouraged speakers to go deep into their chosen issues and were phrased so that they required more than a one-word answer. For this inquiry, we used questions and statements such as:

- "What do you think?"
- "What do you suggest we should do?"
- "Tell me more about . . ."
- "How do you feel about . . . ?"

We probed deeper with follow-up questions, once again without judgment. We were just collecting data. When we got answers, we paraphrased what we heard to make sure we understood.

Then we advocated for our position but did so respectfully by using evidence to make our case and explaining our reasoning. We gave recommendations, making clear what we thought was best. Then we asked for feedback to make sure we had been understood. Some questions and statements we used included:

- "Here is the evidence."
- "I intend to . . ."
- "These are our options, and this is my recommendation based on my interpretation of the evidence."
- "What do you think of these ideas?"

Since this was a training exercise, we weren't trying to resolve actual conflicts. The exercise gave us the skill to resolve one. If your employees in conflict do this with respect for each other, always seeking to maintain a balanced approach, they can begin a dialogue that can lead to an agreeable resolution. This skill can turn an unhealthy conflict into a creative problem-solving discussion. It can give people the confidence they need to go directly to the other person involved when there is a pending conflict. It might even keep people out of your office by allowing them to fix a problem themselves instead of asking you to do it for them.

Conflict and Courageous Leadership

One additional point needs to be made about conflict and confrontation. It has to do with courage. As leaders, we must have the courage to speak up when we have an important and relevant truth that needs to be communicated. Doing so takes courage because we don't want to say something that could be proven wrong. We don't want to be embarrassed or risk damaging our organizational influence. But if we remain silent at such times, we run a greater risk of letting our organization and its people down.

When I first joined the executive team, I was the most quiet and risk-averse member. As time went on, though, I found my voice and realized that it was possible to speak up about difficult subjects without losing face or embarrassing others. In fact, our team expected me to do so and respected me for it. When there was a critical subject being discussed, my test for whether I needed to speak up was if I kept thinking that I should. That sounds simple, but it works. In other words, if I was fighting with myself about whether I should say something, I took it as a good indication that it needed to be said. These subjects were often related to my animal health and welfare expertise, but not always. In fact, when I would bring up a financial or operational concern, it seemed to make a greater impact. To pull this off well takes finesse, an understanding of the issue, knowledge of the audience, and courage. Otherwise, speaking up becomes the sound of just another complaining voice that gets ignored. As one executive I interviewed put it, "Don't be afraid to disagree, but don't disagree just to disagree. Don't go to the worst-case scenario just to get attention."

Having the courage to speak up is always a judgment call. If you see something important that others do not, be humble, be kind, be truthful, but be courageous. Find your voice and speak up. And make it safe for others to do the same.

Just like the diseases we fight in our zoo animals and in our own bodies, conflict is best prevented. Developing trusting relationships by serving others and clarifying roles will immunize us from most conflict. But conflict is part of life. Handled with skill and courage, conflict can lead to good things. This takes a level head, a good dose of self-awareness, and most of all, a servant leader mind-set. By taking the direct approach, preparing for critical conversations, basing decisions on evidence rather than assumptions, and balancing understanding with persuading—and teaching our staff to do the same   we can reach the point of mutual learning that resolves conflicts, benefitting our work relationships and ultimately animal health and welfare.

CHAPTER 7

Honor Staff and Peers

The seven members of our team were in turmoil, huddled together in the kitchen of our host's home in Kruger National Park, South Africa. We had arrived with a dozen crates of equipment just hours before. As a zoo veterinarian, I knew I was about to have an experience of a lifetime. It was my project, and I was the leader. The research trip was to study the effects of a new anesthetic agent named A3080 on hoofed animals, from gazelles to elephants. We had been planning and fund-raising for over a year and would be working there for a month, conducting a scientific study that would involve more than one hundred animals. We had a tight schedule and would be busy every day.

Instead of being excited, however, I was angry. I am not prone to loud outbursts, but I had just exploded and felt justified in doing so. The drug company that was supplying the experimental drug had insisted that one of its veterinarians come along on the trip. It was her responsibility to get the drug to South Africa safely. Since everything would depend on our having the drug supply, she had shipped it early, assuring us that it would be there by the time we arrived. The supply hadn't arrived, though, and no one knew where it was. I was panicking. We had all these people and resources ready, but we had no drug to work with.

What made the situation worse was that the drug company veterinarian was acting flippant about it. In fact, she'd decided to go bird-watching since there was nothing else to do. When I'd challenged her nonchalant attitude, she had picked up our host's phone to call the United States, not considering the time difference, who would pay for the call, or what she was going to say. That did it. I lost my temper, telling her exactly how I felt about her, personally and professionally.

Fortunately, the other veterinarian from San Diego stepped in to diffuse the situation. He simply said, "When I find myself in a situation like this, I make a list. We'll write down what she needs to find out when she calls the United States."

So we did, which got everyone working together to solve the problem and gave me a chance to cool down. By focusing on solving the problem, my San Diego colleague honored both me and the other veterinarian (even though neither one of us deserved to be honored for our actions at that moment). The list that we put together that afternoon provided the structure we needed, giving the drug company veterinarian an outline to use when she called. With that small action, the group once again felt hopeful.

When we want to gain influence in our careers, we usually think first of influencing the high-level decision-makers in our organizations. In doing so, however, we may forget about the importance of our staff and peers. The people we work with are critical to our success in establishing organizational influence. Our support staff members will not be secure, loyal, or fully functional unless they understand that we care about them.

The most influential servant leaders honor their team as individuals as well as a group. The old saying applies here: "They don't care about what you know until they know that you care."

Why the Word Honor?

I choose to use the word *honor* when describing this leadership characteristic because it goes beyond just treating people well. It connotes deep respect.

Honor is a status we can give to others. It builds them up, raises their dignity, and prepares them for a higher level of performance. Honoring staff members means treating them as if it is our job to serve them rather than vice versa. It fosters loyalty and wards off unhealthy conflict. Honor is unconditional and separate from accountability and performance (which we still must address). Honoring others is the essence of upside-down leadership— it is servant-hearted and service-minded.

One of the meanings of honor is to fulfill a debt or an obligation. When we take on a leadership role, we do so with an unspoken agreement toward those who work for us. We are obligated to pay them a reasonable wage and to treat them with honor.

Employee satisfaction surveys usually include opportunities to provide comments, and I was often surprised by the unpleasant comments we managers received about our interaction with staff. The most troubling comments came from those who reported being treated rudely, dismissively, or aggressively by those in authority. When I read those comments, I couldn't help remembering that moment in Africa when I was all those things and more.

This type of behavior is difficult to change, though. It can be rooted in busy schedules, unreasonable demands, emergency situations, and workplace culture. Research on destructive communication in the medical field indicates that it is a widespread problem, particularly for individuals in health care. In a 2015 study published in the UK journal *Clinical Medicine*, nearly one-third of the physicians in three teaching hospitals reported rude, dismissive, and aggressive communication between doctors. The damaging communication was the result of heavy workloads, lack of support, patient safety, hierarchy, and culture. This destructive behavior caused emotional distress, substance abuse, and demotivation. In addition, most junior doctors and other staff with lower status in the hierarchy were treated rudely. In some of the specialties, negative communication was part of the learned culture. The authors of the study said the prevailing thought was that rudeness was a mild word for a mild problem and that resilience should be the response. But this behavior, especially from those with hierarchical power over others, can be damaging and even dangerous. In my experience, it is no less of a problem in zoo veterinary departments.

Separating Honor and Respect from Accountability

Looking back at the situation with the missing anesthetic drug in South Africa, I learned from my mistake. Losing my temper and showing disdain for another person did nothing to help solve the problem. In fact, doing so probably made me look like I was the biggest problem in the room. My colleague took the better approach by showing respect for the individuals on the team.

The drug did arrive two days later, and the study went on as planned. But my poor example as the leader of the team during those tense two days of waiting set a negative precedent, giving the group permission to mistreat and isolate this person for the rest of the trip.

How might I have handled the situation differently? I could have given this person the honor and respect that everyone deserves while still expressing my concern—with my temper firmly in check. This is a key point. We must understand the difference between the honor due to a person and the accountability and consequences due as a result of someone's actions. Affirming and honoring this person's value should have been my first response as the leader of the team. From there, being clear about my expectations would have given us a more successful team experience.

Honor Goes beyond Function

People want to be honored and treated with dignity and respect—not just valued for a function they serve—especially when they have erred in that function. If we consistently treat people with honor, we will have a loyal workforce of people who care about each other and the reputation of their leader.

In thinking about undeserved honor, I can't give a better example than the way one of my first bosses treated me. After training at the San Diego Zoo, I was a veterinarian at the Smithsonian's National Zoo. I worked there for two years, and I enjoyed it thoroughly. But then a job opened in San Diego. I told my boss I intended to apply, and he was supportive of whatever my family and I chose to do. When I was called to San Diego for an interview, he took me to lunch to convince me to stay. He showed respect and no sign of bitterness. He even drove me to the airport.

His greatest moment was on the day I received the call with the job offer. Somehow he knew. As if on a mission he had planned all along, he breezed into my office with a rather tentative smile. Then he shot out his big, rough hand for me to shake and said the words that still amaze me: "Whatever your decision, I want you to know that I respect it and have enjoyed having you as part of my team."

His words were appreciated, but it was his act of coming to me first and without conditions that made me feel honored. It immediately eliminated any anxiety I had over how to handle letting him know I was taking another job. And it set the tone for a continuing relationship that has flourished for thirty-five years since that day. He understood the power he held by honoring me as a person, not simply for the function I could provide for him. Because of this incident and others like it, I hold a special loyalty to him. He continues to be an influence in my life.

A veterinarian, or anyone who is viewed as an authority figure, is in a unique position to bolster the status of others. This recognition will give others a reason to be loyal and engage in the greater vision. One leader I know has a reputation for honoring his close staff by taking every opportunity to communicate that their well-being is important to him. He advises his team members to do the same with their own staff by saying, "It's how we do things here. It's the people that matter." Wouldn't it be great if every workplace were like that?

Honoring your staff is one of the most valuable and underused tools for developing organizational influence. Honoring others helps to humanize the workplace by recognizing that people have value beyond their workplace function. Staff members who feel honored by their superiors will return that honor in the form of loyalty and exceptional results, which build your reputation, credibility, and influence.

CHAPTER 8

Connect with Purpose

When I was the veterinary director of the Zoo, my boss was a kind and generous man. I knew him as the curator of birds, the director of collections, and the director of the San Diego Zoo. He made me feel comfortable in conversation, and I never wanted to disappoint him. I could trust that he would do the best thing for the organization, the animals, and me as an individual. Our CEO placed him in a variety of high-level jobs because of his formidable blend of competency and character traits.

When he was nearing retirement, he was asked to work with the San Clemente Loggerhead Shrike Program. This program sought to increase the population of an endangered subspecies of shrike by using captive propagation techniques and facilities located on the island. It was an approach that the San Diego Zoo was uniquely capable of accomplishing. My boss was stepping in at the CEO's request following years of chick survival problems that were putting the future of the program in serious jeopardy.

He called a meeting of everyone involved, leading with his typical congenial style. He patiently listened to the reports, taking into account the perspectives of all the team members in the room. The information available was contradictory and incomplete. There didn't seem to be a clear reason to explain the poor chick survival rate, but there was plenty of speculation about the many possible causes. Everyone had an excuse ready. The meeting had no direction, no conclusions, and no resolution, leaving everyone with only mounting frustration and pressure.

Then he stood up and went to the chalkboard, commanding everyone's attention. Picking up a piece of chalk, he wrote several numbers from 5 to 30 on the board.

"How many chicks do we need to raise each year to make the program successful?" he asked everyone and no one in particular.

There was a short discussion with no one offering a clear answer. Then, he took the chalk and slowly and emphatically circled the number 30. "This is the number of chicks we are going to successfully raise this year," he told us. He spent the rest of the meeting directing a discussion on how to accomplish the goal. The meeting ended on time and with a huge sense of direction and a feeling of mutual responsibility. Everyone pulled together in their respective roles and did what was needed. There was no argument about what could go wrong or who would be responsible. They all did what they could to reach the goal and help this population thrive. The following breeding season was the most productive one that the San Diego Zoo ever had.

My old boss knew he didn't have the solutions to the problem, but he immediately recognized what the team needed—to be reminded of the "why." Why were they there? Why were they doing this work? Everyone already knew the answer: to hatch and raise an endangered species. They needed a successful breeding season for the San Clemente loggerhead shrike, which would lead to a self-sustaining population. He had refocused the group on their common purpose. That reminded them of their own intrinsic motivation. And everything changed.

A Leader's Number One Job

Motivating people is a leader's number one job. As that story shows, my boss was particularly good at motivating people. He rediscovered the vision and communicated it clearly. I saw him lead other teams in similar ways. He was humble, he cared about people, and he was passionate about animals and their survival. People trusted him. When he stepped up to lead people by giving them a purpose, they followed.

Just like with the shrike team, when a leader reminds people of their purpose, they become more motivated, creative, and productive

What is the best way to motivate?

Strict accountability is one approach and has its place in managing people. But good leaders do not rely on that because it creates a transactional environment that may feel like manipulation. Employees lose motivation when pressured to perform, requiring even closer supervision.

On the other end of the spectrum, some leaders try to gain favor by being overly inclusive, attempting to gain full consensus before doing anything. The effort, then, becomes more about satisfying individual agendas than about satisfying a unifying mission. That often leads to indecision and political wrangling by those who want to influence the leader.

The story is very different for employees who understand their work's purpose. They motivate themselves and one another to do their best. Decisions are easier because they have an agreed-upon purpose. Accountability is easier, almost becoming self-imposed, when people understand the "why."

The Value of the "Why"

Just as my old boss did with the shrike team, effective and influential leaders connect with their staff by fostering clarity of purpose. Effective leaders pay attention to their team members' hearts—their intrinsic motivation—and remind them of a common purpose: the "why."

Veterinarians going into procedures are good at describing the "what" and the "how." We tell staff members what we will do and what we want them to do. We also tell them how we will do something and how we want them to assist. But how often do we take the time to explain the "why"?

The "why" gives context and meaning to a procedure or activity. Sharing the "why" assures those working with us that we have thought through the procedure. It makes it clear that what we are doing is important, necessary, and part of a greater purpose. The "why" connects the vision to the role of animal health and to the task at hand. It reminds people that together we are making a difference. It is another way to honor and inspire staff. And an inspired staff is a productive staff, and that enhances influence at all levels.

Sometimes we veterinary leaders forget the purpose of what we're doing. We can easily get bogged down in the details of complex medical cases. Such dynamic situations require our constant attention to keep track of diagnostic and therapeutic directions. The minutiae can overwhelm the big picture, keeping us from remembering the "why."

The health of our giant panda Shi Shi was one of those complex cases. He had multiple geriatric problems, but one of them was especially worrisome. He would develop epistaxis (nosebleeds) on occasion. The bleeding was usually minor, but we were concerned it might indicate a serious underlying cause. In dogs, epistaxis can be the result of cancer in the nasal cavity. As time went on, the bleeding got worse. After discussing the situation with the panda team and our consultants, we decided we should figure out what was going on. We did not have on-site advanced imaging such as CT or MRI scanners. We either had to bring Shi Shi to a scanner or bring a scanner to him. We chose the latter. What made this so complex was coordinating the schedules of all our consultants (anesthesia, surgical, dental, radiology, and internal medicine), plus our own veterinary department staff. We also had to keep our administration and public relations staff informed.

The CT scan on Shi Shi went well. No tumor was found, but we did discover that the nasal cavity of the panda is highly complex, even more so than a dog's. This complexity made the CT scan very difficult to read. Our consultants recommended everything from doing nothing to surgically exploring the sinuses. We had medical findings to consider as well as animal management and organizational realities to think about.

As the department head and chief veterinarian, I knew it was my job to keep perspective. I struggled to keep the "why" front and center for myself and everyone else. I even struggled with what the "why" was. This elderly panda was no longer a breeder, so he didn't have a role in the sustainability of the population. But we were committed to caring for him. We were pulling out all the stops to determine what therapy, if any, we could give him. There were a lot of eyes on us. Figuring out the right thing to do, with all these factors in mind, was a little disconcerting.

Veterinarians are frequently in this position. They have a lot of demands placed on them. Situations are changing rapidly, frequent decisions must be made, and communication must be flawless.

Our diagnosis for Shi Shi, finally, was epistaxis from hypertension. Our overarching purpose was to provide the best possible care for this aging individual, so that translated into no surgery. Instead, Shi Shi was put on antihypertensive medication. This also began a husbandry training routine that eventually enabled us to collect his blood pressure while he was awake.

I used that example because it demonstrates some of the characteristics of a complex case. As I wrote it, I got caught up in the detail, almost like I did when it happened. The complexity pulled me away from the point I wanted to make . . . which indeed is the point I want to make.

It's easy for us to lose sight of the greater purpose when we deal with complex, high-stakes cases that draw us deep into the weeds. The challenge for effective veterinary leaders is keeping the staff in the loop about the "why" of our efforts. Keeping the big picture in mind, especially in complex cases, is not only important to the team, but it is also essential to providing high quality care.

Discovering Our Values

Our profession lends itself well to inspiring others with the "why." What we do has a compelling purpose and is self-motivating. This is where values come into play.

We all have personal values, and the departments and organizations where we work also have values. The more aligned our personal values and organizational values are, the more we can be of service to our organization and satisfied in our jobs. Discovering our values, aligning our values with those of the organization, and reminding ourselves of the purpose behind those values is the path to successfully motivating and inspiring others to achieve greatness.

So, then, what are values?

Values answer the "why" question. They give us an idea of who we are. They give us a sense of what ought to be. They tell us what we ought to be paying attention to.

Values are different from goals. They don't tell us what to do; they tell us who we are. But they can help us decide what is the right thing to do. Values can be an internal reference point that directs our behavior. They can also help us answer the "what" and the "how" as well as the "why." When we know our values, making decisions is easier.

Since values are based on who we are—as individuals and as organizations—they should be discovered rather than invented. Most of us know what is important to us. Articulating those values in clear and accurate language brings them to the forefront of our minds.

Many leadership books include questions to determine workplace values.

I've found these to be the best ones to ask ourselves and, when appropriate, to ask of our staff:

1. *What makes you most fulfilled and satisfied at work?* These are the things that you find real joy in doing.
2. *What causes you the most heartache at work?* These are the things that upset you the most and become strong motivators for either avoidance or change.
3. *What is your most long-standing passion at work?* This is what you dream about. This is what you wish could happen but perhaps don't dare to act on.

These three questions, when thoughtfully considered, will clear the fog to help you discover your own values.

Aligning Our Values

I did the exercise myself. Then I compared my values to my organization's values. San Diego Zoo Global established organizational values many years ago, and I was fortunate to be part of the team that developed (discovered) those values. So comparing values was relatively easy to do: mine aligned nicely with my organization's values.

These, I came to understand, are my personal workplace values. I clarified each value further with active "be" statements that speak to who I am, not what I should do, since they are values, not goals:

- *People matter*: Honor others. Serve others' needs first. Be honest. Value the team.
- *Animal health and welfare matter*: Advocate for the animals. Be in authority. Sharpen skills. Promote species conservation.

- *San Diego Zoo Global matters*: Be a good financial steward. Be loyal. Be disciplined in using resources. Be generous and giving.

In a Blind and in a Bind: When Values Don't Align

It was 1985. I was a young zoo veterinarian eager to contribute to species conservation and lucky to be part of the effort to save the California condor from extinction. On this particular day, however, I found myself in a figurative "bind" and a literal "blind."

I was part of a three-person team attempting to trap and radio tag the few remaining condors in the wild. We were in a "blind," a plywood box used for spotting wildlife without being seen. We were there for the same purpose: to identify the cause of a precipitous population decline threatening extinction of the species. But there was a bigger issue going on inside the blind that day. It had to do with a decision that could spell survival or extinction of a species. That was the "bind" I was in.

I was sitting between two men who had fundamental differences in their thinking and their values. One, representing the government position at the United States Fish and Wildlife Service, thought the few remaining birds should be brought into zoos for safekeeping, captive breeding, and eventual release when the captive population was sufficient and mortality factors mitigated. He was certain that it was the only solution to prevent extinction. The other man, representing the National Audubon Society, thought the birds should remain free and protected in the wild. He was equally sure this was necessary to protect the habitat. Without the birds occupying the habitat set aside for them, there was little hope that the land would still be available when the birds were ready to be reintroduced. It would be better to let the birds go extinct with dignity, he argued, than to go extinct sitting in a zoo in the manner of the passenger pigeon.

One man's values were based on saving a species regardless of where; the other man's values were about saving the species but only in its habitat. They both had viable points of view. Both sides represented scientific-thinking conservation organizations. Yet on this topic and particularly in the confines of this wooden box, their values were not aligned, their emotions were heated, and the stakes were high. Choosing the wrong path could mean the end of this ancient and magnificent bird.

My job that day was to deal with any emergency medical problem that might occur from either the handling or the netting process, as well as to collect biological samples. We snuck into the plywood blind at dawn and waited. We had to remain alert, talking only in whispers throughout the day. We were there until late afternoon, but we were unsuccessful. In the meantime, I was witness to a conversation that had no resolution for these two men or the organizations they represented. Their values were misaligned, and neither man would accept an argument that ran counter to his values.

Values are strong motivators. They dictate decisions and motivate action. It is difficult for people to willingly go against their values, explicit ones or not. When values are misaligned, the decisions related to those values will be controversial, whether it is within a program to save a species, an organization like a zoo, or work groups within a department.

Misaligned Values in Work Groups

Much as we all wish it wasn't true, some individuals in work groups have values that don't align with those of the group. In a zoo setting, where most staff and employees are there because of a passion for the mission, this may happen rarely. But it happens. When evaluating the impact of misaligned values, it's important to consider your employees' performance *and* values. As a rule, it's simpler to modify performance than change people's values.

It's easy to spot staff members who have both subpar work and misaligned values. They rarely last long in their jobs. It's less easy to spot those whose work is subpar despite their aligned values. If such staff members are willing to go through training or a change of responsibilities to improve their performance, keeping them is usually a benefit.

What about staff members whose work is good despite the fact that their values are misaligned? You may be tempted to put up with them because of their productivity, but in the long run, if their values don't align with those of the group, they can have a devastating impact on the morale of the entire team.

The ideal situation is for all staff members, including leaders, to be productive in their work and highly aligned with the organization and the team in their values. These employees are like precious gold to leaders. They should be rewarded and honored so they become loyal and aware of how valued they are. These are the ones you want to develop as leaders. They will in turn live their values and become positive examples for other employees.

Encourage your staff members to ask themselves:

- What are your workplace values?
- What makes you most fulfilled and satisfied?
- What causes you the most heartache?
- What is your biggest passion?
- Why are you doing the work you are doing?
- How do your values line up with those of your department and the organization?

Connecting your staff with purpose, discovering and aligning your values, and continually reminding yourself and your team of the "why" of your work is the surest way to successfully motivate and inspire others and to have greater organizational influence.

CHAPTER 9

Give Up Control to Gain Influence

In the early 1990s, there was a feverish buildup to obtaining giant pandas from China for the San Diego Zoo. It was quite a remarkable time. The whole Zoo pulled together, and each of us wanted to contribute to the project. We learned a new sense of collaboration out of necessity. It was fun in a high-pressure sort of way.

A PhD behaviorist, who had done the most work with giant pandas from a research perspective, was put in charge of the panda team. Even before the animals arrived, we met regularly as a large group at the Zoo hospital library conference room. The panda team leader sat at the head of the table and was clearly in charge. (This understated and wise man chose to work collaboratively.) Attending this meeting were representatives from the research and conservation team, members of public relations, the Zoo's director, operations managers, and the CEO. We were all working toward a common goal of obtaining giant pandas for our collection and doing it right.

One day, several weeks after we had been granted permits to receive the giant pandas, the subject of quarantine came up. After waiting so long for this historic moment, many of the leaders in the room suggested that the animals could go directly to the exhibit, which would allow the guests to see them earlier and would make the pandas available sooner for behavioral research (which was the rationale for why the permits had been approved). We knew quite a bit about the health of Bai Yun and Shi Shi from our contacts in China. But as a veterinarian, I knew how important quarantine was for the protection of our collection and for the protection of the giant pandas themselves.

Today, we base quarantine duration and biosecurity measures on a risk analysis rather than a rigid set of policies and procedures without evidence to back them up. In the 1990s, however, that risk analysis had yet to be established. When the question came up from our CEO about whether the quarantine could be shortened from the standard thirty days, I decided it was my moment to show that I, as the organization's chief veterinarian, was in control. I quickly and brashly pointed out that since the word *quarantine* is derived from the number forty, the thirty-day duration we typically used was actually a shortened quarantine. We had already achieved a shortened quarantine as per the etymology of the word itself, I said cleverly, thinking it helped prove my point.

I remember the reaction of the team after I made this controlling, pompous statement. No one said anything, including the CEO, but the body language of the group told me that I had just used up a good deal of my trust equity.

In the end, it worked out to be a non-issue: we quarantined the pandas on exhibit, using extensive biosecurity. It certainly wasn't worth my efforts to assert authority and control.

Conflict and Lost Influence

Let's take two examples of an animal management decision.

First, let's say the animal health staff is excluded from the animal management decision for no apparent reason. Based on our knowledge and experience, we have a lot to offer but are not given a chance to do so. We become discouraged and feel insulted that we lack influence in important areas that involve us, so we push to have authority and control over such decisions in the future. But pushing for more authority and control usually backfires, as it did when I tried to exert control over the panda quarantine.

I began this book by explaining that other leaders often view zoo veterinarians in this light. I believe we lose influence and our seat at the decision-making table when we are viewed as roadblocks to progress, simple technical experts with no strategic interest, or arrogant people who believe we deserve to be included because we are veterinarians. How can we change that?

Let's say we find ourselves invited into the decision-making process, though. Most animal care decisions are easily made by consensus, but sometimes there will be a disagreement. When conflict occurs, how do we decide who "wins"? Is it the loudest person? The one who has the director's ear? Ideally, we want decisions to be based on a partner relationship. How can we make that happen?

Most workplace conflicts revolve around a lack of clarity concerning roles and authority for decision-making. For both of these scenarios, the solution can be a change in perspective and a clarification of roles. Successful partnerships are based on establishing clarity—clarity around who makes the decision, who has input on the decision, and what the decision areas are.

That does not mean that successful partnerships are based on equal and identical roles. Rather, partnerships thrive when the roles are distinctly defined. When they aren't, influence and respect are often lost.

A former veterinarian colleague of mine learned about this dynamic early in his career while working at another zoo. His story vividly illustrates how we can lose sight of the "why" when we wrestle for control over authority. He'd reported a severely lame hyena with an obvious fracture to the new curator, who had just been promoted from keeper. The veterinarian always had a good relationship with the keeper, but after the promotion, the curator had become extremely authoritative, desiring almost complete control. When the veterinarian suggested that he needed to anaesthetize the hyena to examine the limb, the curator disagreed, stating that the animal would recover spontaneously. My colleague couldn't believe it. So he played the "I'm the veterinarian" card, thinking his authority in health matters would change the curator's mind. Instead, the curator only dug in his heels more.

The situation became a battle of wills. Three more times the veterinarian tried to challenge the curator's authority by asserting his own expertise. Finally, when the keepers complained that the animal was being ignored, the curator acquiesced and allowed an examination. By that time the fracture was so far beyond treatment that the animal had to be euthanized. The veterinarian openly criticized the curator in front of the staff. But the staff members weren't just angry at the curator's stubbornness. They were also angry with the veterinarian for not figuring out a way to help the animal.

Both the curator and the veterinarian lost influence and respect with the staff, and the animal paid the price for their personal, self-centered struggle. The veterinarian chastised himself for a long time about his ineffective leadership. He decided the experience would be meaningful only if he learned how to navigate future problems better and end the struggle for control. It was a hard lesson, but it changed his entire method of leadership for the rest of his career.

As I noted in my story about the panda quarantine, I also had to learn to overcome my desire for control. The good news is that we can achieve something of greater value by understanding and acting on a key concept.

That key concept, simply put, is: *to gain influence, give up control.*

Although we desire control over high-stakes animal care decisions, what really matters is having overall influence in the organization. To obtain long-lasting influence, leaders must squelch the innate desire for authority and control.

Some people see this as an obvious way to work, and it fits their temperament. Frankly, though, most of us would rather disregard this part of the servant leadership dynamic. It's easy to believe that striving for control is the noble thing to do and the way to ensure the right decision is made. As one of my team members feared in chapter two, giving up control may also seem like an indication of weak leadership—an easy opportunity for others to take advantage of us.

If we wrestle with people for control, however, we will lose valuable influence, trust, and credibility in the long run. Instead, we can choose to respond with humility and respect. We can serve others' needs as well as our own. If we do this, our influence in the organization and with other people will soar. Applying this principle can lead to strong, trusting partnerships with synergistic outcomes.

Giving up control leads to greater influence and better decisions. This happens more quickly than you'd expect. For example, picture two concentric circles. The larger one indicates those issues that concern you as someone who has a stake in the outcome. The smaller circle represents those issues for which you have some influence. The good news is you can increase your circle of influence to be closer to the size of your circle of concern, regardless of your position or title. Like any skill, this takes practice. It takes time and consistency. When coupled with humility and integrity, your experience and expertise can be a powerful source of influence. And the best news is that exerting such influence is entirely under your control, whereas the final decision may not be.

This approach can change a win-lose situation into a win-win situation and a distrusting relationship into a collaborative partnership. When applied by animal care leaders with good intent, the relationship improves, trust mounts, and animal welfare ultimately benefits.

Role Clarity

Let's say you find yourself in a situation where you must partner with a colleague. Once such a partnership arises, before anything else is done, you and the other person should clarify your roles. After that, you can take more practical steps.

Here are the steps that have worked best in my experience:

Identify Decider/Adviser Roles

The first step is to identify and define decision-making roles. This is an important step in achieving clarity. In most circumstances, there are two distinct roles: the "Decider" and the "Adviser."

The Decider is the responsible party and has the ultimate decision-making authority. Good Deciders seek input from those in the Adviser role. They take full responsibility for outcomes and blame no one if things go wrong. In contrast, the role of the Adviser is to influence the Decider. They can change the Decider's mind by providing evidence, interpretation, and recommendations. Their manner must be professional and respectful, honoring the Decider's position.

Veterinarians often find themselves in the Adviser role. They have specialized knowledge and often are the ones who uncover a problem first and in the most depth. By initiating dialogue and providing their perspective, they can be the primary drivers in the decision-making process. Ultimately, the Adviser must support and respect the Decider's decision, though.

It is important to remember that neither role is more valuable than the other; both are necessary for making good decisions. Again, successful partnerships are not based on equal and identical functions. Rather, they thrive when roles are defined and distinct.

Identify Areas of Partnership

The next step is to identify key areas in which the Decider and the Adviser need to partner in decision-making. What needs to be decided? What are the decision-making roles for each party in every part of the situation? This discussion is a critical step in creating clarity and avoiding confusion and lost time.

First, let's explore key decision areas in which the curator is the Decider and the veterinarian is the Adviser. Any such list would include:

- Collection planning
- Acquisition and disposition
- Animal welfare issues
- Husbandry and enclosure design
- Animal escape and recapture
- Regulatory issues regarding animal care
- Nonemergency euthanasia
- Health and disease management practices
- Medical case management affecting sustainability and welfare

Notice the last one—medical case management. You might think the veterinarian should be the Decider. But often that is not the case. Consider an okapi with an abscess on its flank. The question between the veterinarian and the curator is this: immobilize the animal or watch it for further problems? As the Adviser, the veterinarian has an opportunity to be influential by providing a sound evidence-based recommendation (without political maneuvering or forcing his or her own way). As Decider, the curator stays in

103

control of the collection and any implications on sustainability for the rare species, tasks that are both part of the curator's larger responsibility. Even though you know what is best medically, the curator may decide differently due to bigger factors. You have to be willing to let go of control.

Sometimes, of course, the veterinarian is the Decider and the curator is the Adviser. That list might include:

- Quarantine and biosecurity
- Preventive medicine
- Emergency medical care
- Basic and daily case management
- Egregious animal welfare issues (USDA role as the veterinarian on record)
- Regulatory issues related to health

You probably agree that the veterinarian should be the Decider for most of these. But remember, the Decider takes responsibility for the outcome of the decision and actively seeks input from the Adviser. It can be a huge responsibility to have that authority. Regarding animal welfare, the curator has the major responsibility, so in most cases, the curator needs to be the Decider. In the unlikely event that there is an egregious animal welfare issue, however, then the roles switch—the veterinarian's USDA-mandated responsibility as attending veterinarian means that the veterinarian must become the Decider.

I recently heard an interesting twist on the Decider/Adviser methodology that shows how valuable and versatile the concept of giving up control can be. One of the young veterinarians told me that he willingly took on the role of Adviser when he would have traditionally been the Decider. Zoo veterinarians are specialists, but I see us as the ultimate generalists, since we work on all species and all problems. One thing we become extremely good at, though, is anesthesia. In zoo practice, our procedures almost always involve anesthesia, so when it comes to choosing the method of anesthesia, the veterinarian is the obvious expert and clearly should take on the Decider role, with the keepers being the Adviser. This young veterinarian, however, decided to turn that thinking upside down. He took on the role of Adviser regarding anesthesia, allowing the keepers at the hospital to make the final decisions on such matters. For example, the keepers would decide whether to use an intravenous injection after restraining an animal or to dart the animal in the stall.

By giving the keepers the choice and responsibility, the veterinarian found that they took a greater interest in the outcome. The keepers could use their greater knowledge about that individual animal to anticipate how it would respond. What do you think that did for this veterinarian's influence with these keepers? My guess is it ultimately strengthened the entire team.

Adviser Drives the Process

You can have influence without being in a position of authority. As zoo veterinarians, we often do not have the authority to make decisions, but we can drive the decision-making process and exert influence in important ways.

This is also true with medical doctors. I had an experience with a doctor who was a master at being an Adviser. He demonstrated that he could drive the decision-making process without being the Decider (who in this case was me). A few years ago, I was at home doing my morning workout when I started having an unusual feeling in my chest. It was painful but not severe. I showered and shaved and decided I'd better tell my wife, Robin. We agreed that it would be smart to get it checked out. When I mentioned chest pain to the admissions clerk, we were ushered into a room and I immediately had an EKG. There was no doubt about it. I was having a heart attack. After an ambulance ride to the nearby cardiac care hospital, I found myself trying to convince the cardiologist that this was a mistake. I didn't have the risk factors for coronary artery disease. He assured me that I did, being a male over sixty with family history.

I began to relax, though, when I saw how skilled this man was at serving his patients. I started to listen to him and saw how he drove the conversation. Despite my situation, I recognized that he was using the very technique I had discovered about how to gain influence with decision-makers. Without making an issue of it, he clarified roles up front. He expected Robin and me to be fully in charge of deciding what was going to happen next.

First, he explained to me in language I could understand what they had found. He knew I was a veterinarian, called me doctor, and spoke using basic medical terms. He then explained my situation to Robin in lay terms. Second, he explained the significance of the findings and what they could mean to us now and in the future. Third, he gave us options. The options included evidence from scientific studies about which was most effective, along with associated risks. Finally, he gave us his clear and unbiased recommendation, which was to perform a cardiac angiogram with angioplasty and stents where needed. He gave me information about the type of stents available because there were consequences I would need to know in making my decision. He did not, however, tell me other details such as catheter size or the type of contrast he would use. Those were medical decisions he alone could make because they did not have implications for me down the road.

Robin and I asked a couple of questions and briefly discussed our options. Before I knew it, I was in the recovery room with my family around me and a nice stent in my circumflex artery.

This cardiologist was a professional who quickly earned my trust. He had the character to know his role and the knowledge to drive the decision while allowing us to be the Deciders. He gave us enough information to make a good decision. And he gave us his firm recommendation, which we were eager to hear. Thus, there was no conflict between us. We felt like partners solving a problem together rather than being forced to blindly trust that the guy knew what he was doing.

That's a personal example.

Here is a professional example based on a case I had as a practicing zoo veterinarian. This case involved a juvenile male bonobo (sometimes called a pygmy chimpanzee) who had a respiratory infection. In this case, I was the Adviser and the primate curator was the ultimate Decider. We performed a physical examination under anesthesia. We collected blood samples for evaluating infection, performed radiographs of the chest, collected a percutaneous aspiration of the mass, and did a physical examination.

Based on our findings, we knew we had several options, but there were management consequences for all of them. It was up to me as the veterinarian to drive the decision-making process because I had to implement the decision and I had the key medical information for that decision.

Through experience, I had learned to follow a simple process to work with the animal care decision-makers so that we could make a good medical/management decision together. It looked something like this:

1. Provide a *summary* of the findings in nonmedical terms.
2. Give a relevant *interpretation* of the findings.
3. Provide reasonable and viable *options* without bias (three options, for instance).
4. Give a firm, evidence-based *recommendation* that makes use of all the medical and management information.

For this bonobo case example, then, the process went like this:

1. *Summary*: We discovered a soft swelling in the region of the neck just below the larynx. The radiographs also showed the soft tissue swelling in that region, and the blood work revealed a mild infection.
2. *Interpretation*: The findings revealed an air sac infection with an accumulation of thick pus in the air sac. This was likely a result of an upper airway infection that would not resolve on its own.
3. *Options*: 1.) We could begin treatment with a long course of antibiotics based on sensitivity testing of the aspirate. 2.) We could open the air sac surgically and manage it as an open wound until it healed. 3.) We could leave it alone and see if it healed on its own.
4. *Recommendation*: We recommended option 1, since we knew it would cause minimum disruption to the group compared to option 2 and had a reasonable chance for success. We also chose option 1 because this did not appear to be a chronic condition yet and we felt there was a good chance option 1 would resolve the problem. If it did not, we knew we may need to progress to option 2. Doing nothing would likely lead to a chronic condition that could create further problems, so we did not recommend option 3.

Presenting the problem in the decision-making process in this fashion often leads to further dialogue between the two parties and collegial agreement. This can minimize unhealthy conflict, build trust and healthy relationships, and ultimately lead to a better decision based on evidence rather than personalities and political maneuverings.

Giving up control to gain influence is always going to seem like a paradox. Even so, it is a powerful servant leadership principle, useful for those without positional authority who want to have influence as well as those who are called to continually work with colleagues in establishing clear roles. It's an important principle to understand and apply in our work and home environments. It achieves better results and, more than not, is the right thing to do in serving others.

To gain influence, give up control.

CHAPTER 10

Allow the Team to Develop Standards

I remember the morning I looked up from my desk at the Zoo and welcomed our new hospital manager into my office for our weekly meeting. I was looking forward to it, as I did all my weekly one-on-one meetings with my managers. Each conversation was unique. The managers set the content of the meetings. I was there to listen and occasionally offer suggestions or redirect their efforts. These meetings also gave me a glimpse into what was happening with the people and the animals. I often discovered critical things that I was missing.

Our hospital manager arrived with her usual mug of coffee, but today she was also holding a notepad. On her mind was a topic that would lead to a big change in how our department viewed accountability. She said she wanted to ask me a question. She remembered that, during her job interview, I had emphasized the "people part" of being a manager. I had wanted her to understand that character and behavior were as important to me as competency.

She took that information very seriously. In the time since she had been hired, she had noticed some behavior problems in her area. A few individuals weren't treating each other with respect and did not seem to think it was critical to the job. She'd noticed that we had nothing in writing that spelled out what behaviors we actually expected from them. So she asked: "How do I hold people accountable for their behavior without some sort of written expectations or standards?"

It was a question I had not considered before.

She explained she did not have any trouble holding people accountable for their technical performance. She had been a technician herself and would frequently get feedback about that kind of performance from the veterinarians and other coworkers. But standards for behavior seemed vague and difficult to assess. Everyone seemed to have their own ideas about how to treat people. She already understood how much I valued respectful and professional behavior in our department. She knew I wanted us to be the example for the whole institution—that I wanted other departments to wonder how we got along so well and were so productive in our service to others.

Her question about how to monitor and measure those behaviors in her staff was the genesis of our team's behavior-based standards. She was right: we needed clear, written standards. We also had to figure out the best way to write and implement them. She and I took the concept to the other managers on my animal health team. At our next meeting, we began the work that led to our behavioral standards.

Creating Behavior-Based Standards

Working with the animal health managers, we followed this process to create behavior-based standards:

- First, we started with San Diego Zoo Global's code of conduct, called the "Rules of Engagement." We needed to be in alignment with and give support to the organizational culture, so we began by basing our standards broadly on the organization's values.
- After choosing seven of the behavioral standards for our needs, we rewrote them to clarify expectations and ensure accountability. We put the phrases into our own words so they would make sense in our work environment. For each standard, we wrote a catchphrase to make the concept more relevant. We also wrote clarifying questions to help identify specific, desirable behaviors.
- We took the draft to each of our department work groups (veterinarians, technicians, keepers, laboratory technicians, and administrators) for their feedback, additions, and edits. We wanted this to be their document and not just seen as a manager's tool.
- Finally, we shared the finished document at our monthly staff meetings. We also shared it with our human resources staff and our executives.

To be most effective, behavior-based standards should reflect the unique nature and values of each workplace. Below is an example of how we turned one of the code of conduct rules for San Diego Zoo Global (SDZG) into a behavior-based standard for our department.

SDZG Code of Conduct Rule: Use Your Words Wisely
- Our rewording: Think before you speak.
- Catchphrase: My words and nonverbal messages affect those around me and our work environment.
- Clarifying questions: Am I being respectful? Am I phrasing my message in a positive manner and offering solutions? Am I addressing the

issue directly with the person involved? Do I express gratitude whenever possible?

Here are our remaining six behavior-based standards along with their catchphrases:

- Take responsibility: By holding myself accountable for my actions, there is no one else to blame.
- Work effectively: When I use my time wisely, the entire workplace benefits.
- Build excellence: I bring out the best in myself and others.
- Harmonize: I can achieve harmony when I balance my work and personal priorities.
- Create joy in the workplace to relieve stress: I can help create a pleasant and respectful workplace.
- Make lasting memories: I create a legacy of learning, innovation, service, and leadership.

Again, these are examples based on our work environment; I offer them, though, as a model.

Measuring Behavior—Personal Responsibility

Being accountable for ourselves, and fostering it within the teams we lead, shows responsibility. Such accountability gives us credibility with others and builds our larger influence.

But holding ourselves and others accountable is a tricky business. A set of rules can convey that we care more about rules than people. That perception invariably leads to opposition. In fact, I have heard it wisely stated that "rules without a relationship lead to rebellion."

As leaders, it is tempting to save these standards and use them only when someone misbehaves. So we asked the animal care managers: How can we avoid that? How can we hold people accountable and still serve our staff's needs? How can we uphold high standards without damaging relationships?

Part of the answer came from our experience of clarifying roles with our curator colleagues, as discussed in the previous chapter. Just like we needed clear roles and responsibilities when working with curators and others, we also needed clear expectations for accountability with our staff.

Clarity is the key. Without clarity, holding people accountable for desired behavior is both difficult and unfair. Without clarity, people tend to do what is right in their own eyes. And if the leadership and the culture allow such self-serving behavior, confusion and conflict will be the result. Everyone will feel like a victim.

As we thought about what makes a healthy work environment, we decided that creating an environment in which everyone takes personal responsibility for their behaviors would be most effective in the long run. Our approach was to create a culture in which our behavior-based standards were identified and consistently practiced. Accountability, then, would become part of the culture.

Ideally, staff members would be interested in examining their own behaviors, learning new behaviors, forgiving others, and owning the results. In other words, no one would feel like a victim and everyone would feel like a responsible partner.

In my weekly meetings with the hospital manager, we often spoke about how we could use our new standards. We decided that, in addition to using our standards when things went awry, we should also use them to reward and acknowledge employees who exemplified the desired behaviors. Soon, the standards became important in our recruitment and hiring process as well. I went over them during interviews of the top candidates to give them an idea of the culture they would be joining.

With agreed-upon, behavior-based standards, a common language emerges for acceptable behavior—and a culture of shared, personal accountability results. For our department, the clarity was wonderful.

Sustaining the Standards

One aspect of this process, however, we didn't execute so well. To sustain behavior-based standards, the leader must provide a venue for repetition and reminders. We never found a consistent way to do this before I retired. If it isn't done, though, eventually the standards could fall away.

One solution to sustaining standards may lie in how a particular service-based company—known worldwide for extraordinary customer service—dealt with keeping its standards high. At the Ritz-Carlton hotel chain, legend has it that one night a bellman once took it upon himself to stay all night at a hospital with a guest who had an emergency appendectomy. Such behavior is part of their culture. Rather than workers serving guests, the employees consider themselves ladies and gentlemen serving ladies and gentlemen. The lauded hotel chain hires people to partner in this vision, not just to fill a function. Even a good company culture, however, needs constant reinforcing. So to sustain their standards, the leaders have a tradition. They make a point to review one of their behavioral standards in their group meetings at the beginning of each day. The managers and supervisors take turns teaching the standard as well as sharing examples of someone who exemplified it particularly well. A practice such as this gives everyone an opportunity to apply and reinforce the behaviors and develop leadership skills as well.

Reinforcing standards on a continuing basis can help your department maintain any behavioral standards you and your team create, but only if it is done in the context of honoring and valuing your employees and their commitment to the organization. Doing so offers road markers for everyone concerned. It reminds us as leaders that how we conduct ourselves is of utmost importance in what we do and broadens the influence we have in the organization whose mission and vision we love.

CHAPTER 11

Encourage Unity through Diversity

One of the greatest privileges of being a zoo veterinarian was that I could observe, up close, animals that most people have never even seen or knew existed. I have handled the thick, long tail of a snow leopard. I have peered into the mouth of a pelican. I have removed a foreign body from the furry, padded foot of a polar bear. I have examined the beautiful and complex eye of a chameleon. I have witnessed the incredible adornment of a male bird of paradise in flight. I have looked through an endoscope at the compartmentalized stomach of a douc langur, which is adapted for digesting leaves. I have placed my hands inside the abdomen of a koala to repair an intestinal obstruction.

I took many things for granted in my career, but I never got over being awestruck by the beauty, diversity, and intricacy of animal life and the honor of seeing it close up and intimately. It still amazes me how every part and component of an animal's body (e.g., extremity, organ, cell type, biochemical reactions, genetic code, natural behaviors) function together to serve the animal as a whole.

To see a California condor flying is an incredible sight, so different from the common turkey vulture's weaving and rocking path through the air. The first time I saw a condor in flight, the stability of its large, flat wings reminded me of those of a Cessna airplane. When I looked more closely, though, I could see that each primary flight feather on the condor's wings was working independently to adjust the flight. Then there were the things I didn't see, such as its well-developed cerebellum, which coordinates all the complex movements required to fly.

When I think of what a condor can do, I am envious. I've always wanted to fly. But all that remarkable wonder falls apart when, for example, a condor suffers from lead poisoning. The toxicity affects various parts of the nervous system, reducing the function of other body components. Those parts that are directly unaffected are eventually affected indirectly.

Every animal functions as a unified body with separate parts that are all vital to the whole. When one part doesn't function correctly, the entire animal will be in distress.

Unity through Diversity

So it is with people working in teams.

A successful team is a unified entity made up of individuals who are each vital to the group. These two concepts—unity and diversity—might seem to conflict. Which is more important for team success? Unity of purpose? Or diversity of strengths and talents? We might have exceptional individuals on our team, but no matter how much individual talent there is, a team will succeed only when the players have a unified purpose. At the same time, success can be achieved only through diversity—using each person's diverse skills, talents, training, and experience. So the best answer to the question is that for a team to be successful, it must have both.

Diversity itself is a source of strength and unity in a team. I'm not talking about tolerating differences but embracing diversity with vigor, for no matter how much we want others to be like us, uniformity of thought and function is not helpful for a team. We might have unity on a team with members who are alike in talent or temperament, but the team will be less strong and less effective than a team made up of diverse people who have learned how to be cohesive in purpose. Diversity might seem to be counterproductive, posing potential problems with so many different points of view, but through diversity, we can have freedom and independence and still be effective—*if* we work for a common purpose.

With a shared purpose, a team benefits from all its diverse skills and talents. And that establishes unity.

Think about the condor. Are the wings the most important part of the condor or is the cerebellum? That seems to be an irrelevant question since both parts provide integral functions for the animal. The condor needs all its parts to be healthy, each functioning for the good of the whole. The brain and nervous system may be in charge, much like a leader of a team is, but without the rest of the condor, there is nothing to oversee, and therefore being in charge means nothing. The brain has no more value than any of the other parts of the body, since it has no value apart from the whole. Some parts, like a condor's wings, are more prominent and given more attention, but even the wings are wholly dependent on the integrated functioning of organs and other parts.

The same is true with veterinarians or any other professional. No matter how significant we think we are, our importance comes only from our collective efforts. Zoo veterinary leaders depend on their teams.

Enemies of Teamwork

In my leadership research, I've read about many "enemies of unity" within a team. Experts talk about such problems as lack of interest, uncooperativeness, inflexibility, and stubbornness. In the zoo veterinary world, I've found two enemies to be the most powerful destroyers of a team's unity through diversity: arrogance and gossip.

Arrogance

Arrogance is defined as an attitude of superiority manifested in an overbearing manner or presumptuous claims or assumptions. The self-important leader probably thinks something like this: "My idea of a team is having a lot of people do what I tell them." Put into practice, however, that thought destroys morale and unity. It devalues diversity and other team members. It is the opposite of being a servant leader. One person's time is no more valuable than another team member's. As veterinarians, we may have special skills or a license that makes us the only ones who can have certain important roles on a team, but that does not make us inherently more valuable than any other member.

Each of us is significant and valued. But no matter how valuable we may think we are, it is only our contribution to the whole team's efforts that sets our value.

Gossip

Gossip is defined as a casual or unconstrained conversation or report about other people, typically involving details that are not confirmed as being true. The key phrase in this definition is "about other people." Only secondarily does it matter whether what we are saying is true or not.

A slightly broader definition of gossip is anything negative said about a person to someone who is not there to speak up for himself or herself.

Once, I was tempted to complain to my staff about a decision made on the executive team. The decision involved how resources should be distributed during a period of lower than expected institutional income. I thought that some of the departments were sacrificing more than others. If I had followed through with complaining about the decision to my staff, they would have supported my complaints. We would have shared a moment of agreement and conviction. But even if my complaints were valid from my perspective, what good would they have done in the long run? I'm sure you can imagine how unproductive and divisive such complaints could have been for the unity of the organization as a whole. Besides that, even those in my department would likely have questioned my professional integrity afterward. That is what gossip does.

A good test to determine whether something is gossip or not is to answer this: Would I say the same thing in front of the person in question?

We can control our own urges to gossip, but our teams will also be prone to venting or spreading information by gossiping. How does a leader or a team member handle such moments productively?

I've learned that if peer-level team members are gossiping *to* you, they will likely gossip *about* you later. That's a clear reality check on the situation and its consequences. The answer, then, is not to participate. Tell the gossiper you are uncomfortable talking about someone else without that person being present. Then redirect the conversation. Doing so is a way to assert your personal influence in a positive way. If you are in a position of leadership, I urge you to take a hard stance against gossip. Because of its damaging effects to a team, gossip is not a behavior to tolerate.

Zoo Leaders' Perspectives

In my interviews of zoo leaders, the issue of diversity and unity came up repeatedly. Many zoo leaders saw veterinarians as highly trained technical experts who had diverse talents but were separated from the organization as a whole. As busy as veterinarians are, and as long as it takes them to master clinical medicine, they need to put their best efforts into their specialty. It's understandable how spending time and effort getting to know the inner workings of the whole organization can seem overwhelming and take veterinarians out of their comfort zones. However, a talented veterinarian acting separate from the organization is like the left wing of a condor choosing to work independently. It's beautiful in its own way but useless for the entire bird.

It is tempting to remain a technical expert only. But the better, more effective way to lead is to be alert to opportunities to partner with others outside our area of expertise.

One zoo director said this: "If you are successful and respected as a veterinary clinician, you will be asked to solve all sorts of problems that are not clinical." You can say no, but taking advantage of those opportunities will lead to other opportunities to exert your influence in the organization. When the situation arises, follow the advice of another director: "When an organizational problem comes up, just raise your hand, volunteer, and say, 'I can help you with that.' And do it in a positive way." Your organizational influence will spiral up.

Another leader said: "Be a part of the cult of the cause instead of the cult of the individual." Veterinarians can assert themselves to use their strengths in new ways and participate in the bigger process. That's the theme of this book—and the long-term welfare of the animals in your care depends on it.

Being part of a successful and highly functioning team is one of the most satisfying experiences an individual can have. We can achieve this by seeking value in each of our coworkers and realizing that a diversity of skills and talents is the source of team strength and unity.

Let's admit that others have strengths we don't. Let's generously use our strengths to compensate for those who are weak. And let's offer our time and our interests to the larger cause of the organization when the opportunity presents itself.

When diversely talented individuals work in synergy, miraculous things can happen.

CHAPTER 12

Develop Team Members into Leaders

One of the most compelling reasons for my leadership quest has been the hope that others in our profession will follow sound leadership principles and will extend their influence into the future. Several have done that and done it their own way. Li Desheng is one such example.

As part of the agreement that came with the two giant pandas from China, Li visited the San Diego Zoo for a six-month period in 1997 to learn and to share with us his knowledge about giant pandas. In 1999, I worked with him in Wolong. We were in our second year of a three-year biomedical survey of giant pandas in China. Li was a young veterinarian at the bottom of the ladder who had been chosen to work with pandas. He spoke English well, and he was engaging, humble, hungry to learn, and seemed to understand and enjoy people. He stayed in our home for two weeks so I could help him with transportation. He was a joy to have in our home, even offering to cook us a traditional Chinese meal. I took him to our local upscale grocery store to get supplies. The odd selection of produce and meats that he wanted gave the store manager and the entire staff a fun challenge. After he spent hours in the kitchen, we ate and ate.

At work, Li studied at every opportunity. He was clear about wanting to learn so that he could aid in the conservation of giant pandas and help his team. He bolstered his Chinese veterinary technical training with whatever he could glean from our library and through the medical cases we saw. When he returned to China, he consulted with us over complex medical cases, which he handled with considerable technical and interpersonal skill. Through all this, I recognized that he was a future leader—the right person to share our knowledge about zoo veterinary medicine, which he could use for the benefit of giant pandas in China.

Now, nearly twenty years later, Li Desheng is the deputy director of the Wolong Giant Panda Protection and Research Center. In addition to overseeing animal management and science, he is also in charge of finance and administration. Li has achieved a high level of organizational influence and is making a mighty impact on giant panda conservation in China. This is what matters to me. I'm proud to have played a small part in his development as a leader in our pivotal field of saving endangered species.

As zoo professionals, it is our responsibility—and in our best interest—to develop the people around us into leaders. How is that done?

When I tried to answer that, I only came up with more questions:

- Do we just let it happen randomly, or should we be intentional about it?
- If we are intentional, on whom should we focus? A select few? Or can anyone serve as a leader?
- How do we begin to develop staff members into leaders?
- How do we prepare ourselves to lead?

The answers to these questions will ultimately determine our legacy, extending or not extending our influence beyond our own careers.

Be a Good Model of Leadership

I don't know if you are aware of this, but you are being watched as you go about your day as a zoo veterinary leader.

You model who you are and what you do every day. This example filters through your entire staff. If you expect certain behaviors, you must give your staff an example to follow. You cannot give what you do not already have.

Take a moment to review the character traits we've discussed so far: a servant attitude, humility, the ability to put people first, the ability to build trust, honoring others, and having a clear purpose. These characteristics of an influential leader are the antidotes to the insecurity and desire for power that is so prevalent in the workplace today. The most important qualities are the ones you'd like to see manifested in your team. But that will rarely happen unless you are reflecting those characteristics yourself.

Prepare Team Members to Lead

I love to hear stories of rank-and-file team members choosing to do the right thing. One of our technicians, for example, tracked long-term medications for animals in the collection. He was aware, as most of us were, of the dangers of using a flea product on a cat that was designed for only dogs. In reviewing the prescriptions for our animals, he noticed that a dog housed with a cheetah—a practice proven beneficial for the well-being of the cheetahs we used in our educational programs—was being given a flea medication indicated for dogs only. He worried that the cheetah was being exposed to a medication that could possibly be harmful. He didn't know for certain anything harmful was happening. He just knew of the overlooked threat.

The technician reported the suspected problem to the veterinarians with confidence and without fear of criticism. Then he announced his intentions to change the long-term medication to a product that could be used in both cats and dogs, if the veterinary staff approved. One of the veterinarians responded and quickly approved the change. The technician's proactive approach ensured that the animals were treated appropriately.

One of the best aspects of this story is that the necessary action happened quickly, without drama. The issue did not fall between the cracks waiting for a decision or for someone to take responsibility. A threat to animal health was averted because the veterinarians were humble enough to encourage the technician to develop as a leader. And as the story spread, the confidence in and influence of the entire department grew.

What was it about this individual and his environment that made it possible for him to take responsibility, be a leader, and grow his personal influence and that of the work group? My guess is that his bosses, who focused on animal health, had encouraged their team members to be watchful for any problems. The technician probably felt safe pointing out an oversight by his bosses, knowing they'd approve of his potentially lifesaving catch.

Here is the underlying truth: if we want sustained influence in our organizations, we need to invest in others and help those around us find courage to become leaders themselves.

Developing leaders is not just for professionals or succession planning. It is essential for smooth daily operations and successful outcomes. In such an environment, all employees become leaders. Regardless of rank, they take responsibility and assume authority for their area of expertise. In doing so, they are being trained as future leaders.

Here are a few tips to help those around us practice leadership.

Use Empowering Language

Often, as authority figures, we feel the need to look like we're in charge, to give directions, and to be the source of knowledge. This authoritative approach, however, holds others back from developing their leadership skills. Even more, it leads to confusion concerning daily tasks and assignments. Staff members abdicate responsibility and avoid making decisions. Errors become more prevalent.

In these environments, employees often use language that shows their dependence and insecurity. No doubt you have heard these weak phrases in the workplace:

- "I don't know what you want me to do."
- "What should I do about . . . ?"
- "I was told not to . . ."
- "I have no authority to . . ."
- "I need your permission to . . ."
- "It's not my job."
- "Tell me what you want me to do."

As leaders, we might be tempted to read into these phrases that our authority and expertise are needed. But encouraging staff to use such language promotes dependency and a lack of responsibility.

There's a better way. The simple practice of using empowering language can reduce this dependent behavior. It can be done through word choice and good timing.

First, invite your staff members to use phrases that reflect accountability. This method empowers people. It can transform insecurity into confidence, build trust, and reduce errors. When confronted with a problem, a staff member's use of empowering phrases—encouraged and modeled by those in authority—shows budding leadership potential.

To signal your confidence in their leadership potential, encourage your staff to use phrases such as:

- "I intend to . . ."
- "I plan on . . ."
- "I will . . ."

Using this approach to empower can play out in a variety of situations. Here is one way the process can work:

1. A staff member sees a need for action and knows what to do. (This should occur regardless of that person's position in the department.)
2. That staff member, using empowering language, tells the responsible party (usually you, the boss) that he or she intends to take action.
3. You, being the responsible party, acknowledge the intention. You may ask clarifying questions. Then you agree to the action or make a change as needed. Roles are crystal clear. Authority and responsibility are in their proper context. The staff member no longer feels micromanaged. Delegation is effortless.

This process redirects the authority to the person who is the source of the information—that is, to the staff member closest to the needed action. It decreases mistakes. It eliminates confusion over who is going to act. And it reduces any time that may be wasted waiting for you, the veterinary leader who is busy with so many other responsibilities, to make a decision.

In other words, staff members who can assert themselves will take full advantage of their knowledge and experience while still allowing other staff members to check their reasoning. These employees grow in their jobs and practice leadership in real-world situations.

This reminds me of one of our hospital managers and some problematic doors in the hospital's hoofed stock area. This manager, a longtime employee, had worked for us as a hospital keeper, a veterinary technician, and finally a hospital manager. She was part of the design team for the Paul Harter Veterinary Medical Center at the Safari Park, the largest and most sophisticated zoo animal hospital in the world, which opened in 2001. The hospital is a beautiful place and well designed. But after we moved in and began to use the new facilities, we found that the large shift doors between the hoofed stock pens were designed with undersized pulleys. Over time, the doors became difficult to move, putting our hospital keepers at risk.

This manager's handling of the situation shows how effective it can be to encourage one's staff to lead. She did not ask her bosses what they wanted to do, putting the problem on us. She understood she could take the lead and find a solution. Instead of using phrases such as "What should I do?" "It's not my job," or "Tell me what you want me to do," she used phrases such as "I plan to," "I intend to," and "I will."

She got a bid for the repair, which was considerably higher than what we had budgeted. She knew the importance of getting the doors fixed quickly, though, so she didn't give up. She did more research and made a workable plan. Then she reported that plan to both her supervisor and me. Her plan was to get the work done in phases, starting with the next budget period. She was confident that her plan would allow the work to stay within the year-end budget, even though expenses would go over budget occasionally for the period.

The doors got fixed.

Instead of asking me to work through a solution without having firsthand knowledge of the problem, she handled it. I was fully informed of her plan and had the opportunity to ask questions. Thus, the action happened without delay. She took personal responsibility for a problem her team members were facing. She checked her reasoning with others, which increased support and decreased the likelihood of mistakes. Everyone involved had the opportunity to weigh in on the decision, which bolstered their credibility and influence. And she grew as a leader.

This example shows how the language we encourage our employees to use can change the way people work. The use of empowering phrases can signal a staff member's intention to take responsibility. Making this work takes courageous leaders who aren't afraid to support decisions by those who are close to the action.

Focus on Strengths

My team and I were driving our veterinary truck in the South Africa field exhibit at the Safari Park one morning on our way to anesthetize a springbok that was going to be shipped to another institution. On the way through the exhibit, we encountered a male ostrich in full courtship display. He dropped to the ground, opened his wings, shook each one alternately, swayed his head, and otherwise looked rather foolish. We couldn't help but shake our heads and laugh. One of the students with us remarked, "They sure aren't the smartest animal around." No one could disagree, and we'd all heard it said before about ostriches. But I thought it was an unfair judgment about this bird.

So I said, "Apparently, they are as smart as they need to be because they are well suited for what they do."

The ostrich is a successful species because of its strengths, which include size and speed. Perhaps a comment about an ostrich's intelligence is harmless, but it points to a common mistake managers make as we try to develop our team's leadership skills. We naturally notice our staff's weaknesses, and we often focus on fixing them while ignoring their strengths. Research by the Gallup company shows, however, that focusing on our strengths is far more effective. We commonly hear, "You can be anything you want to be if you just try hard enough." This sounds inspiring, but research shows this is not true. A more accurate statement is, "You cannot be anything you want to be, but you can be a lot more of who you already are."

A strength is the ability to consistently provide desired performance. A talent is a natural way of behaving or thinking. By investing the time and the effort to practice and develop our talents, we can build our strengths. There is a multiplier effect when we invest in our talents. The effort we invest is like the force needed to get a flywheel in motion. Once it gets going, the momentum sustains it. Small efforts yield large, sustainable results.

In contrast, when we focus on our weaknesses, resistance is strong, so our efforts yield meager results. Instead of developing momentum, constant effort is required to sustain change. As a result, big efforts yield small, unsustainable results. Remember that when you set out to change someone's behavior.

Just to be clear, we all must do things that do not use our strengths. We cannot and should not avoid doing those things. However, it is a poor investment to focus on them all the time.

When our animal health manager's team participated in an evaluation using a popular strength assessment tool, I was surprised by the diversity of strengths in the group. It was helpful to see whose strengths overlapped and whose complemented others. That is the value of a team. Different strengths yield robust results. When my wife, Robin, and I took the assessment, none of our top five strengths overlapped. We've been married for forty-two years, so having different strengths must not be a bad thing. Her top strength shows that she likes to talk. She is good at connecting with people. She can ease any social situation. She loves the challenge of meeting new people, putting them at ease, and winning them over. My top strength shows that I have faith in the links between circumstances, believing that there are few coincidences. You can probably guess that we see things differently. We make good use of those differences, though. We both appreciate connections with people. She is good at making them, and I enjoy learning about people's lives and the wisdom they have gleaned from their circumstances. Although I'm trying to be better at meeting new people and I'm learning to speak more quickly to put them at ease, this will never be a strength for me as it is for Robin. But I can readily improve my strength of looking for the root cause of circumstances and finding a common link that explains them.

It's common to compare our own strengths to those of others. With the ostrich, it was easy to choose intelligence—presumably a strength found in humans—as a standard by which to judge, while ignoring the bird's stronger attributes. This type of error happens when we compare others' weaknesses to our strengths and judge their weaknesses as faults (e.g., ostrich intelligence). At the same time, we excuse our own weaknesses (e.g., size and speed) as being a result of our circumstances.

This is a trap we can easily encounter, but it breaks down trust on a team. This error can occur between any work groups, including veterinarians and technicians. A technician, for example, may find it easy to organize for procedures but have no patience for the veterinarian who does not provide a list of equipment needed for the next day's procedures. The veterinarian may find it easy to think of the possible causes for an animal's problems but be disappointed that the technician did not anticipate what equipment was needed. That's an error of thinking on the veterinarian's part. And it comes from focusing on one's own strengths and expecting others to have the same strengths.

To prevent this error, we should practice focusing outward, grasping the idea of strength in diversity on our team. When we do that, we seek to understand more than we expect to be understood. Instead of concentrating on people's weaknesses, we respect our staff members' strengths and see them as complementary to ours. The basic idea of having a team is to meld strengths so we can be stronger together than apart.

Hire the Right People

I remember the first person I had to fire, and the experience taught me a tough lesson about how to hire the right people. It happened thirty years ago when I became a department head at the San Diego Zoo. The person was a licensed technician who worked in a specialty practice and was quite pleasant in the interview. I asked job-related questions that she answered adequately. I did not think it was necessary to check references. We needed the help desperately and immediately, so we hired her and started training. She turned out to be a poor fit for rebuilding our department, and the termination process was miserable for everyone involved. I even second-guessed myself and wondered if I had been fair. The few times I had to let employees go after that went much better technically, but emotionally, they were just as bad. The lesson I learned about hiring was this: we needed to develop a strategy to identify team members with the right character and fit for us.

Developing such a strategy requires an extraordinary amount of time. Being able to recognize the right people is a challenge, so it helps to have a defined strategy. Firing someone is a terrible end to a long and difficult journey of counseling, performance plans, weekly progress meetings, and consultations with human resources. When we hire a new staff member, we impact our existing culture. Depending on the person selected, the culture can be strengthened, weakened, or otherwise altered.

We need the right people "on the bus" to develop into our leaders. A hiring strategy helps us select the appropriate employees. My tendency was to hire for an immediate need—i.e., so we could fill the schedule with skilled labor. Doing so seemed relevant and reasonable, but it was a shortsighted approach that I paid for later.

Regardless of the position being filled, I should have looked at the big picture. I now know that everyone needs to be a leader regardless of job title, so I should have looked for leadership qualities and characteristics. I also should have looked for someone who could be a team player. These characteristics are harder to sort out than technical expertise or a publication record. Nevertheless, taking the time to ask probing questions and dig deep is always worth the effort.

Make that next hire count. If I were still in the position to develop a team from scratch, I would choose the following approaches to identify, hire, and develop staff members. These hiring strategies, gleaned from two excellent leadership books noted in the appendix, can help clear the fog surrounding the selection process.

The first is called the three Cs of hiring, which are character, competence, and chemistry. Character is first on the list because it is the most important. Good character is difficult to determine in a short interview. Therefore, it is vital to take the time to get to know a person. If you have doubts about a person's character, you should look elsewhere. Don't be fooled into thinking you can smooth out someone's character with time or coaching. Getting references from past employers or associates is essential.

Once a person has qualified for a job based on character, then a thorough evaluation of the candidate's competence is in order. Credentials and specific skills may come into play.

Finally, look for chemistry, which is another word for fit. This covers both how you feel about working with this person and how he or she would fit into your desired culture. Some people think it is unfair to choose someone based on your chemistry. But it is not only fair, it is also the kind and compassionate thing to do. It is a disservice to hire someone who will not fit with the culture or the other staff members. Using the three Cs can help you be more confident in your hiring process and increase your chances of finding the leaders of the future.

To the three Cs I would also add three virtues.

The first of these virtues is *being humble*. This virtue is so important that I devoted an entire chapter to it earlier. Carefully crafted behavior-based interview questions can help shed light on a candidate's humility. Asking about weaknesses, accomplishments, and when things go wrong can give you an indication of whether that person is an attention seeker, self-directed, or individualistic—all of which would indicate a lack of humility.

The second virtue is *being hungry*, which is another way to describe someone who is a hard worker, self-motivated, and looks ahead. By asking about a person's general work hours, you might save yourself a surprise later. Although work/life balance and family life are important, a candidate who focuses on the number of work hours required may be someone you should pass up.

The third virtue is *being smart*. This type of intelligence refers to interpersonal relations. In this context, a smart person is someone who understands human nature, likes people, and has good self-awareness. Ask about a time when the candidate demonstrated empathy toward a coworker. That question will yield important information. Having empathy for others is a key indicator of success in working on teams. It's important to hire someone who understands the value of that.

Develop Top Leaders

Martin Luther King Jr. famously said that anyone can be a leader, because anyone can serve.

As leaders, we must expect leadership from those we hire and those with whom we work. But the second part of his statement explains the type of leader he was talking about: one who serves. We need to develop this kind of leader—a leader who wants to serve—at all levels in our organizations, from managers to frontline workers. As zoo veterinarians, we must select the right people to follow in our footsteps: young veterinarians who have the desire to serve.

At the executive level, where the stakes are the highest, developing people who can serve has even greater significance. Executives will have great demands placed on them and face the temptation of power. Those who rise to this level with a servant leader's attitude will be of great value to their organizations and to the mission stated in the veterinary oath: to serve both society and the welfare of animals.

It takes time and commitment to develop servant leaders, and sometimes the best opportunities for teaching come at unexpected times. For instance, I always appreciated having staff members stop by my office to talk. I know this goes against much of the time management literature and popular thinking, but I considered those moments to be gifts rather than intrusions. Sure, there were times when I was on a tight deadline, concentrating on a complex subject, and I could not be interrupted, but for the most part, I did not want to discourage anyone who felt the need to talk to me.

If I was with someone in my office, I refrained from answering the phone or doing anything that took my attention away from my visitor. I learned to stop what I was doing, push back from my desk and computer, make eye contact, be a good listener, and ask questions.

I wish I could say I practiced these servant leader traits naturally or intentionally. I think I learned them because I was conditioned to benefit from the interruptions. For example, a few years back, when the associate director of veterinary services would come into my office, I knew I would learn something valuable. She was the kind of leader I wanted to see at San Diego Zoo Global. She was humble and smart and had a great capacity to get things done. She was quickly promoted to supervising the veterinarians at the Safari Park. The subject matter of her visits varied considerably. It could have been a complicated medical case, a staff issue that was troubling her, or something she just thought I needed to know. Whatever it was, I welcomed the contact.

When she had a problem, I learned that she wanted me to listen and let her resolve the problem herself. The best I could offer were questions to help her probe the issue. Our brief discussions usually concluded with her saying something like, "This is what I intend to do." Then she would tell me her plan. I had the option of changing that plan or giving feedback, which I rarely did. Looking back now, I can see that she was growing toward a position of greater responsibility. Together, we were developing her into a leader who could take my place when I retired. And that is exactly what happened.

The staff members with the best potential to be top leaders need more than just a casual office visit and mentoring, though. They need to see us, their leaders, be an example of how to develop into a high-level leader.

CHAPTER 13

Develop Yourself into a High-Level Leader

Anyone can be a leader and exert organizational influence. I have provided evidence in this book that I hope has convinced you. In fact, we could probably debate whether a high-level executive has any more influence than a skilled servant leader who is an hourly worker. But no one can dispute the immense responsibility that top leaders have and the impact their decisions have on an organization. These leaders are the example others follow. They set the direction and tone.

This chapter is written for individuals who feel called to be high-level positional leaders and want to lead with a servant's heart. The following story describes an event in my leadership journey that changed me, making me acutely aware of the heavy but essential burden of responsibility those in leadership positions carry.

In 1996, after years of delay, the San Diego Zoo received permits to import two giant pandas for a long-term research loan. The planning for the actual transport of the two animals took months of political and legal wrangling. Finally, plans jelled for a September transport. The pandas were to travel from the Wolong Giant Panda Breeding Center in Sichuan, China, to Shanghai. Those of us from the Zoo were to meet the animals in Shanghai and accompany them the rest of the way to San Diego.

The animals arrived uneventfully in Shanghai, accompanied by a Chinese veterinarian and keeper. The male, Shi Shi, had been born in the wild, rescued after being severely injured, and brought back to health. He was a mature male of unknown age. Bai Yun was a young female who had been the first giant panda born in Wolong to survive to maturity. Both animals were a source of pride for the people in Wolong. The pandas were unloaded at Shanghai Zoo overnight and were scheduled to fly to San Diego the next day. That afternoon and evening, there were celebrations and official ceremonies to mark the occasion. Then the responsibility for transport officially shifted from the Chinese to those of us representing the San Diego Zoo.

The next morning, the animals were crated, put on a truck, and transported through Shanghai traffic to the airport. I was concerned about transporting them in September, knowing that temperatures in Shanghai could still be unfavorably warm. We found a relatively quiet place in the freight terminal where they could be in the shade. The activity in the freight terminal increased, however, as the freight was being prepared for loading onto the 747 afternoon flight. It got warmer and warmer and noisier and noisier where the animals were being staged. The plan was to load all the freight onto the plane and then load the two pandas last. Six of us—chief operations officer, curator, animal care supervisor, Chinese liaison, veterinary technician, and myself, the veterinarian—waited together with the pandas, accompanied by a representative from the insurance company who was there to represent their interests.

Because of customs requirements, only the animal care supervisor, veterinary technician, Chinese panda keeper, and I were allowed to stay with the animals while they were being loaded. The others in our party had to board the plane with the rest of the passengers. The animals were loaded quickly, and then the passengers boarded the plane. As soon as he could, the insurance representative joined us in the freight area of the plane with the pandas. The temperature in the freight area had begun to rise quickly. Although the animals had been kept in the shade, the rest of the freight had been sitting out in the sun and was now releasing heat inside the airplane.

That's when I realized something was wrong with Shi Shi. Bai Yun was responsive to her familiar keeper and was even interested in eating bamboo. But Shi Shi was unresponsive and was panting continuously. We did all we could to help him, including blowing fans into the crate to try to cool him down. Nothing was working. The insurance representative was clearly worried. He insisted on hearing what we were going to do.

I was worried too. I didn't know what to do. As a veterinarian, I knew I was there for several reasons. The most obvious reason was to deal with any unforeseen health and welfare issues that might arise. As a representative of the San Diego Zoo, I was also there to show that the Zoo was providing the best care possible. My decision would impact not only my reputation but also the Zoo's. The pressure of the moment was overwhelming.

That's when the insurance representative said, "You have to tell them not to let this airplane take off. We have to unload Shi Shi and find out what's wrong."

I tried to keep a clear head, remembering my roles and my training. My role as an animal advocate told me not to risk taking the animal off the airplane, as the insurance representative was insisting. My training as a veterinarian told me to diagnose the problem and provide the appropriate treatment. I was awestruck by the power I had to stop or at least significantly delay the takeoff of a fully loaded commercial aircraft.

Getting the data needed for such a decision and diagnosing the problem was going to be difficult. I could not take Shi Shi's temperature, so I could not be sure whether the panting and unresponsiveness were signs of heat stroke. We discussed Shi Shi's personality and how he usually responded to stressful situations, and it seemed possible that he had just shut down. I had to decide which would be the best course of action—unloading him or getting him up in the air so the pilot could cool down the freight area. Unfortunately, a clear answer evaded me.

In my role as veterinarian, I knew that no one but me could make that decision. That's why I was there. Veterinarians are trusted to make decisions in the best interest of an individual animal. But my veterinary training and subsequent experience had only given me only a rudimentary understanding of animal behavior in general. I had not had specific training in assessing animal behavior or welfare. To make this decision, I could only rely on my knowledge of diagnosing physical ailments.

All these thoughts went through my head in a few short minutes. I had to decide, and I had to do it quickly.

In the end, I realized that the right decision had to be based on the individual's welfare and not on fear or external pressures. I made a calculated gamble that Shi Shi's unresponsiveness was a behavioral response to his situation. If I was right, it was in the panda's best interest to get the plane in the air as quickly as possible so he could cool down.

The plane soon taxied down the runway, preparing for takeoff. When it rose into the sky, the temperature inside the freight area dropped. After about forty-five minutes, Shi Shi suddenly began to move, look around, and start to eat. We were all relieved. He made the rest of the trip without further incident.

I'd made the right call. With what I knew at the time, though, it could have gone either way.

Making that decision during Shi Shi's transport from China was perhaps the most dramatic moment in my zoo veterinary career. It helped me to grow as a leader and begin to see things differently.

Zoo veterinarians have many opportunities to learn how to make quick, high-pressure decisions for the benefit of individual animals. However, my other role that day—to be a representative of the San Diego Zoo and to look out for the needs of the organization rather than my own needs—required a broader skill. That skill takes time, training, and intentionality to develop. Success in developing that skill leads to a broader perspective that will enhance organizational influence and open doors for positions of high-level leadership.

The fact that you have read this far tells me you not only have the ambition to be a leader at a higher level but also feel a calling to use your expertise to be as influential as you can. I want to give you an overview of ways you can boost your success as an expert animal care specialist and also develop your leadership potential. These suggestions can help you prepare for opportunities to be involved in high-level, far-reaching decisions.

Preparing to Be a High-Level Leader

From my extensive interviews with zoo leaders, I learned a great deal about how zoo veterinarians can prepare for influential positions. There are four points worth reviewing.

Develop a Broader Perspective

The most consistently expressed point was the need for a broader perspective. Technically competent veterinarians who desire more organizational influence should step out of their roles as experts in veterinary medicine and gain experience with broad organizational activities. There are many ways to accomplish this, although they all take time away from clinical activities.

Both director and veterinarian interviewees mentioned that putting veterinarians on the executive team or in regular, direct contact with the CEO had a positive effect for both parties. Doing so encourages veterinarians or animal care specialists to think and act more like senior executives or owners. Doing so also gives the CEO access to someone trained and experienced in complex problem-solving and situational analysis.

One CEO put it this way: "Simply making this veterinarian a VP made him a far, far better manager of his team. When we worked on the institutional plan, he was very thorough. He was one of the best thinkers because he looked at it with the left-brain thinking of the clinician."

Acquire Basic Financial Literacy

Any zoo veterinarian or other animal care leader who has the chance to be part of executive decision-making needs to have basic financial literacy. Executives are expected to be able to read and understand an organization's financial reports. When I was on the executive team at San Diego Zoo Global, we would review the financial statements after each period was over. When I first joined the executive team, I was suspicious that finances, rather than the needs of the animals or conservation, were setting the direction of the organization. I came to realize, however, that I had fallen prey to a common misconception. Finances were a critical tool to help us evaluate the health of the organization. They were not the driver of it.

I learned this slowly. At the beginning of my time on the executive team, our chief financial officer would review the financial report in detail at the meeting. We called it a "deep dive." There would be a few questions and a little pressure on those who were behind on their numbers, but that was it. The executive team took it all in passively. Then our CEO and CFO decided they wanted to take the deep dive to a different level. Each executive team member was assigned a different financial period and had to present the analysis and lead the discussion. In other words, the financial review shifted from a passive to an active exercise for each of us. I learned a lot more that way since I had to understand the reports to make an effective presentation. And it may not be a coincidence that our organization's financial position consistently improved after the executives took an active role in reviewing the finances. During this fundamental financial review, team members brought their own emphasis and interpretation to the presentation. This gave me the opportunity, when it was my turn, to explain some of the financial details pertaining to my area.

Through this process, I came to understand the value of a financially healthy organization in achieving our mission of animal care and ending extinction. I think the other executives were a bit surprised that a veterinarian would take as much interest as I did in the financial health of the organization. As I attained a higher level of financial literacy, I improved my credibility and influence in other matters as well.

Leverage Expertise with a Service-Focused Heart

Zoo veterinarians and other animal care leaders should learn how to use and leverage their expertise in preparation for a high-level position. By this I mean using their expertise to benefit the organization and its people. For example, we can identify disease risks such as avian influenza or Zika virus and put them into perspective for the organization as a whole. Doing this with a servant's heart will lend credibility and engender trust. If zoo veterinarians and animal care specialists learn to offer their expertise using the servant leadership actions in this book, their influence can soar.

Expand Business and Leadership Expertise

Finally, anyone desiring to become a high-level leader should consider additional, broader training beyond the DVM and board certification. This can be as simple as short courses on leadership, finance, and business or as comprehensive as an executive MBA program. Leadership training to develop top leaders for the zoo profession is so important that the Association of Zoos and Aquariums (AZA) has a professional development course that covers some of what we've discussed and much more. The American Veterinary Medical Association (AVMA) and the American Association of Zoo Veterinarians (AAZV) also have opportunities for leadership training.

Gaining Organizational Influence: Animal Welfare as a Science

I could have been much better prepared for the dramatic moment when I had to decide about Shi Shi's health and welfare. In fact, I've never forgotten how much I could have benefited from having a better understanding of animal behavior to objectively assess and measure welfare.

Veterinarians are expected to make big, high-stakes animal welfare decisions. One of the greatest values that executives see in their veterinarians, per my interviews, is their role in animal welfare. We need to be more prepared, not only for ourselves and the animals but also for the institutions we represent. And we need to do it in a collaborative fashion.

But how?

Fortunately, with the modern zoo's greater emphasis on the science of animal care and welfare, we have the chance, and the obligation as leaders, to learn more about this discipline. Since that day I spent on the Shanghai runway with Shi Shi, animal welfare has grown as a science with its own set of principles and methods. Veterinary medicine is rooted in animal welfare, but the science of animal welfare has advanced in different directions from what veterinary medicine has traditionally covered.

Established in 2000, the AZA Animal Welfare Committee defines animal welfare as an animal's collective physical, mental, and emotional states over a period of time, measured on a continuum from good to poor. The

AVMA has a strong focus on animal welfare based on principles of medical ethics and animal care, but its approach is different from that of animal welfare science. Animal welfare scientists devise scientific techniques for measuring animal welfare from the animal's perspective rather than from our own.

Although veterinary medicine and animal welfare science differ, there can be remarkably influential synergy when the disciplines work together. As a veterinarian, you have the potential to create avenues between the animal welfare scientists and the veterinary departments—unchartered avenues that can produce remarkable results.

Organizational Partnering Opportunities

Through my interaction with animal welfare scientists and knowledgeable animal care staff, I've come to believe that zoo veterinarians can, and should, play a valuable leadership role in animal welfare programs. Even the very name of the discipline—animal welfare—calls for our involvement.

Animal welfare is one of the reasons I became a zoo veterinarian. Like all veterinarians, I know what it takes to care for animals well and the consequences of not doing so. But this makes me susceptible to basing my decisions on emotional conclusions rather than evidence gained by stepping back and observing.

That is one of the many ways zoo veterinarians can learn from animal welfare scientists. Veterinarians can only benefit from broadening their focus beyond physical well-being to include the animals' whole well-being, including their psychological health. That is part of the animal welfare scientists' field of study.

Animal welfare scientists can benefit from zoo veterinarians as well. With their individual animal perspective, veterinarians have a common bond with frontline keepers. This gives them the opportunity to educate the keeper staff about using evidence to describe an animal's welfare.

Veterinarians can also provide a conduit to senior management. A veterinarian in a smaller zoo may be one of the few people on staff who has training in the critical appraisal of scientific literature and can look for solutions to problems using an evidence-based approach.

The veterinarian's regulatory role is also critically important. In the United States, the Animal Welfare Act places significant responsibility on the attending veterinarian. Animal care staff members at most zoos interact closely with USDA Animal and Plant Health Inspection Service (APHIS) regulators, but regulations put the ultimate responsibility and authority on the zoo's attending veterinarian.

The USDA has a long-trusted system of accreditation so that a properly accredited veterinarian (a role distinct from that of an attending veterinarian) can certify animal health as if he or she were a government employee. No other zoo employee position offers these qualifications. Zoo veterinarians who take on this role with a servant's heart (i.e., seeking to serve the organization rather than to use the power for self-interest) become highly valuable to their animal welfare colleagues. They have a huge opportunity for gaining respect and influencing the organization.

By working together in synergistic partnership, zoo veterinarians, animal welfare scientists, and animal care staff can increase their organizational influence, protect their organization's reputation and assets, and ensure that the animals under their care thrive.

Organizational Partnering Example: The Animal Welfare Panel Story

The best way to explain the benefits of working together in such a partnership might be to tell the story of the Animal Welfare Panel at San Diego Zoo Global: how it was developed, why it came to be, and how we partnered to influence the ongoing health and welfare of both the animals and our organization. The process was unique to our organization, but the principles may be useful to others with the same goals.

It's a story in which animal welfare experts—animal care staff, scientists, and veterinarians—worked together to influence the direction of the organization. It's also a story about persevering beyond the inherent emotional nature of animal welfare and refusing to be derailed in our mission.

Animal welfare has always been one of San Diego Zoo Global's top priorities. Over the last decade, there were numerous animal welfare efforts working independently of one another. But our CEO wanted assurance that the animals were receiving the care they needed. He challenged the animal experts on the executive team to find a way to measure animal welfare in a meaningful way. It was a wise and relevant challenge, though more difficult than I imagined.

Our group went to work. We reached out to our animal welfare scientist and associate curator for animal welfare, and we put together a workshop to help bring our leaders up to speed about zoo animal welfare science. The workshop made animal welfare an organizational priority and promoted continuing investigations.

Then in 2011, San Diego Zoo Global unveiled a new strategic plan called Lynx 100. This plan boldly proclaimed that animal health and welfare was our greatest priority. It called for a system to assess the effectiveness of animal welfare efforts and to identify a mechanism to locate and correct problems. From Lynx 100 came the idea for the San Diego Zoo Global Animal Welfare Panel. The idea was to ensure that each animal under our care had the best life possible.

The partnership—between a veterinarian, a welfare scientist, and a curator—carried with it some organizational influence, but we needed to get broad organizational feedback and support for the program.

Two big concepts won us the support we needed to move forward:

1. The processes would all be evidence-based, going beyond emotions and politics.
2. The panel would be advisory to the curators so they would stay in control of the collections for which they were responsible.

In early 2013, the Animal Welfare Panel was given a charter based on the design we had created and modified by feedback. Late that year, we planned a six-month rollout. The rollout would culminate in a spring 2014 launch to introduce the panel to the entire organization. It involved an extensive communications plan that provided key messages to all employees. An important part of the rollout was to gain the executive team's approval and support. Once we did, this would no longer be a grassroots effort. It would be the heart of the organization.

We created a formal mission statement (which was similar to our original wording). The mission of the San Diego Zoo Global Animal Welfare Panel, we explained, was "to ensure that each animal under our care thrives and has the best life possible."

Then, with the executive team's blessing, we were ready to help with any animal welfare concerns. We wondered if we would hear few or no concerns from the Zoo employees, as happens in many zoos. We also wondered, given all our efforts to make our existence known, if we would be inundated by submissions. We did not have to wait long. Our first submission arrived three months after the launch.

The concern was about Chuck, an older southern white rhinoceros at the Safari Park. Chuck was well represented genetically and was no longer needed as a breeder. He was being held in a boma enclosure because he was destructive when put out in the big exhibits. He had some enrichment but no companions. The concern was submitted anonymously.

The way the concern was handled is an ideal example of the value of the process. The Animal Welfare Panel contacted the curator responsible for the animal and shared the concern. The curator met with interested keepers, and together they brainstormed solutions. The curator showed his power-under-control, service-focused character by accepting responsibility and seeking the input of those involved. This humble interpretation of his role as curator became a model for all subsequent concerns, showing the other curators to look for evidence, deal with their own emotions, and call on the keepers and other stakeholders to investigate an issue together.

Based on these discussions, the curator decided to introduce Chuck to a post-reproductive female northern white rhinoceros in a large enclosure without other rhinos. The Animal Welfare Panel endorsed the plan. The outcome was that both animals bonded and displayed positive indicators of welfare.

This response came from the keeper staff:

> *It has been just over one month since the conclusion of Chuck's case. . . . Please know how wonderful it is for all of us to know that the Animal Welfare Panel is a real tool for change when change is needed. Thank you for giving us hope in effecting change for our charges. And thank you for giving Chuck a better life.*

The curator's successful response set a precedent. It gave the panel influence by teaching the keepers (and the panel) how to use the concern process properly, applying the evidence-based approach, and honoring the keeper staff by listening to them.

Flush with our first success, we began to fine-tune the panel's efforts. Our scientist and curator were not satisfied with the current ways welfare was being evaluated. We were adhering to the "Five Freedoms," five points of animal welfare for livestock husbandry that had been developed in the 1960s. By the 1970s, the Five Freedoms had been adopted by veterinarians and organizations worldwide, including most groups battling animal cruelty such as the ASPCA.

In a nutshell, these well-known freedoms are:

1. Freedom from hunger or thirst
2. Freedom from discomfort
3. Freedom from pain, injury, or disease
4. Freedom to express (most) normal behavior
5. Freedom from fear and distress

Our team noted that these were "freedoms from." Instead of negatives, however, we wanted to emphasize positive indicators of animal welfare. For instance, many people who see a jaguar pacing in its enclosure judge it as poor animal welfare, and it may be. But what should the jaguar be doing instead? What positive indicators can we look for and encourage?

As I was walking back to my office early one afternoon, I ran into our animal welfare curator. He is the kind of guy who always has a bounce in his step, and that day he was bouncing higher than usual. He was expressing the joy of creating something new and significant by partnering with others.

"We figured it out," he said. "Instead of giving animals five 'freedoms from,' we came up with five 'opportunities to thrive.'" That immediately made sense to me.

The "Five Opportunities to Thrive" are based on research in animal welfare science. They point out positive indicators of welfare and can be used to evaluate the welfare of individual animals. Now they have been incorporated into the animal welfare concern process to help evaluate welfare. The five opportunities are:

1. Opportunity for a well-balanced diet: fresh water and a suitable,

species-specific diet provided in a way that ensures full health and vigor, both behaviorally and physically

2. Opportunity to self-maintain: an appropriate environment including shelter and species-specific substrates that encourage opportunities to self-maintain

3. Opportunity for optimal health: supportive environments that increase the likelihood of healthy individuals as well as rapid diagnosis and treatment of injury or disease

4. Opportunity to express species-specific behavior: quality spaces and appropriate social groupings that encourage species-specific behaviors at natural frequencies and of appropriate diversity while meeting the social and developmental needs of each species in the collection

5. Opportunity for choice and control: conditions in which animals can exercise control and make choices to avoid suffering and distress and make behavior meaningful

The story of the Animal Welfare Panel is still being written by others at San Diego Zoo Global since I retired. It is moving forward and breaking new ground—even offering Animal Welfare courses through the online San Diego Zoo Global Academy. The continuing partnership it fosters between colleagues in different branches of the animal care division raises everyone's influence at the highest level of decision-making—both within the departments and across the organization itself.

I believe that the critical factor in its success lies in the servant leader approach we took. We built and maintained trusting relationships and listened to feedback. Our relationships were solid enough for us to avoid most conflict, enabling us to use our expertise, based on sound science, to make the panel relevant and useful to the organization. Most of all, our willingness to work synergistically with other disciplines for the greater good broadened our influential leadership and gave us a unique "opportunity to thrive."

Good Animal Welfare and Good Leadership

All of us who work in zoos have a responsibility to the animals in our care. Therefore, we also have a responsibility to influence our organizations to keep animal welfare as the top priority. Seen this way, good leadership and good animal welfare have a lot in common. Just as the animals we care for need individual care and attention, so the people we work with need us to be humble leaders who value relationships and honor their needs as individuals. When we lead this way, great things can happen.

The specific needs of the people we lead and the animals we care for may be different, but our responsibility to serve them is the same. And the best way to serve them is to prepare ourselves to lead at a higher level no matter where our careers take us.

CHAPTER 14

Look to the Future: Becoming Right Side Up

S an Diego Zoo Global's hospital at the Safari Park is a showplace. It was designed and built with much forethought. Although I had nothing to do with the design and planning, I always enjoy giving tours to friends or dignitaries. No matter how much I build the place up ahead of time, it never fails to impress people.

At the beginning of the tour, I always pause in front of the pictures of our past zoological medicine residents. By the time I retired, about a dozen of those pictured had finished the program. Each of those pictures represents a person who dedicated three years to a program to learn to be a zoo veterinarian. It is a rigorous program that expects a commitment of heart and mind. Those people are the future leaders of our profession, and we helped to forge their abilities and their character. Standing in front of that wall of pictures is an emotional experience for me.

Most of those pictured on the wall are board certified by the American College of Zoological Medicine. Accomplishing this is extremely difficult.

It is an all-encompassing career goal, requiring young professionals to put their lives on hold for years. It has become the measure of the success of our residency program.

But becoming board certified must not be the finish line. One successful candidate, now a high-level leader, described a surprising feeling after passing the final test. "I thought I should feel elated, having made it to the 'pinnacle,'" he explained. "Instead, I felt an emptiness, thinking, 'What now?' I then tried to fill the emptiness with being the best clinician ever, feeding my competitive nature, and it took the next ten years to slowly realize that wasn't the answer either, that I had to look beyond myself. And I've been lucky to find happiness and joy in others' success at work and at home as well and in helping others find this path more quickly than I did."

This bright and capable veterinarian found joy in being the kind of leader I challenge you to become. Leadership done in service to others is satisfying and exhilarating in ways that are difficult to describe.

As with any profession, becoming a successful zoo veterinarian requires more than just technical knowledge. Most of the zoological world's veterinary residencies, however, are geared toward selecting and training for technical competence. They are much less focused on developing character and relationship skills. Somehow, it seems we expect bright young veterinarians to pick up leadership skills on the job or through some late afternoon chat with one of their mentors. It would be far better for such residencies to include leadership training as an intentional part of their curriculum.

This comes with trade-offs, though. Any training takes time—time that is already committed to clinical work. Becoming a high-level leader eventually means reducing or eliminating your clinical work. For me, that was a hard decision. It gets to the core of what it means to be a veterinarian. At first I wondered, am I still respected as a clinician if I am no longer doing clinical work? Or is it a natural transition as I grow in my career?

Such a decision requires knowing and keeping your eyes on the "why." Being a career clinician is a noble choice, if that is your desire. Zoos need dedicated, experienced, and wise career clinicians. Leadership skills, in this case, will still be valuable for effective communication and relationship building.

If your desire is to have influence, though—with an impact on ending extinction, wildlife conservation, or animal welfare—you must develop refined leadership skills. Such skills are required for you, the veterinarian, to be valued and effective on a higher decision-making level—to be seen as an essential partner rather than a sidelined expert.

I see hopeful signs that our profession is gaining momentum toward that kind of leadership. The residents we have recently trained are hungry for leadership knowledge and experience. This generation seems to understand better than previous ones the importance of these skills. These residents understand our species conservation mission and want to have a personal impact. They know veterinarians have more to offer beyond technical expertise. They realize that it is only a lack of leadership skills—more than even a lack of technical skills—that will limit their impact and influence.

Looking back to the day in 1987 when I quit my job, I now realize that experience was a great gift to me. It was the day I began my journey. From that point on, I sought to understand leadership and be a different kind of leader. I found I had mentors I could emulate. I discovered what it takes to make changes in myself and to influence others. Through this journey, I learned that traditional, controlling leadership is really what is upside down and that it is working against us. A different kind of leadership—serving others' needs first, being humble, cultivating relationships, building trust, remembering the "why," holding ourselves and others accountable, and nurturing others as leaders—is the right-side-up way to grow influence and achieve results. It may be a road less traveled because it takes more effort and goes against the prevailing wisdom, but that road delivers us where we ought to be: where people matter and animals thrive.

As this book concludes, I want to remind you of two overarching themes that represent the path and the destination of that path.

First, remember that anyone can be an influential leader regardless of position. You can have immense influence without authority. You can do that by serving others, being humble, and discovering—and passionately pursuing—the "why." Positional leaders do have additional responsibilities, which demands more authority, but beware of taking advantage of that authority if you are in such a position. Instead, treat your staff and peers with honor. Serve their needs first, and don't expect them to serve your needs.

Second, remember that high-level technical expertise alone won't earn you the right to have broad organizational influence. Step out to step up. In other words, be willing to broaden your perspective. Care about the health of the entire organization by serving its needs over your own. Act like you have the interests of an owner, not the entitlements of a hired hand.

The path is clear: serving others. The destination is reachable: broad influence to stand up boldly for what is good. Although this seems upside down, isn't it really the way you would want it to be?

Influence is a powerful tool for accomplishing great things. How we lead and influence others becomes our reputation and a measure of our career success and significance.

In the end, what do you want your career story to be? Make it intentional. Start writing it now. Chances are, that story will be about people—the ones you served and influenced along the way.

Acknowledgments

I am indebted to the leaders who allowed me to interview them for this study of zoo leadership. They include Lisa Marie Avendano, Ford Bell, Beth Branning, Paul Calle, Leigh Clayton, Bob Cook, Mike Crowther, Jeanette Fuller, Lewis Greene, Rob Hilsenroth, Lauren Howard, Sharon Joseph, Dennis Kelly, Larry Killmar, Matt Kinney, Palmer Krantz, Nadine Lamberski, Linda Lowenstine, Michael Mace, Bob McClure, Eric Miller, Pat Morris, Mick Musella, Doug Myers, Jackie Ogden, Jeff Proudfoot, Geoff Pye, Bruce Rideout, Dwight Scott, Mark Stetter, Meg Sutherland-Smith, Scott Terrell, and Bob Wiese.

I thank the corporate publishing division of San Diego Zoo Global for their amazing support and interest in this project. Georgeanne Irvine, in particular, provided expertise, direction, and encouragement, especially through the project's final phases. I also appreciate the behind-the-scenes leadership efforts of Yvonne Miles. Betsy Holt, publisher with Beckon Books, skillfully made edits to achieve a professional finished manuscript.

I thank the American Association of Zoo Veterinarians, its members, and its leaders. It is a close-knit group of professionals who have an unusual bond through their compassion for animal life, a strong ethic, and extraordinary technical expertise and training. I count dozens of them as personal friends—many with whom I have grown old and others who are still young with tremendous leadership potential. Eric Miller has been a great influence to me since we met as veterinary students at the Los Angeles Zoo forty years ago. Bob Cook has been a peer mentor since early in our careers and has enriched my thinking about our profession and how we lead. I thank Geoff Pye, Scott Terrell, Leigh Clayton, and Rob Hilsenroth for showing us the importance of developing leadership skills for our careers and profession.

The quality of the people in this organization makes me proud to say I was a zoo veterinarian.

I am grateful for the team of animal health managers who were by my side during the last several years of my career. I thank them for making me look better than I really was. They did the practical and hard work of unifying, in philosophy and practice, the Safari Park and San Diego Zoo animal health departments and the disciplines they represent (veterinary medicine, nutrition, and laboratory science). They were PhDs, veterinarians, and technicians by training but leaders and trusted confidants for me personally. The team included Nadine Lamberski, Meg Sutherland-Smith, Pat Morris, Mike Schlegel, Kim Williams, Laura Keener, Jeanette Fuller, and Tracey Mumby.

The people in the departments I was responsible for kept me going as well. The jobs they have dedicated their lives to are difficult. These compassionate people were faced with the best and the worst of life and death every day. But they never stopped trying to do what was right. Their dedication and hard work continually motivated me to earn their trust and the right to lead them.

The specific people in my departments who influenced the content of this book are too numerous to mention. I must, however, name a few. Nadine Lamberski, the one chosen to follow me as corporate director when I retired, handled the transition with grace and respect, for which I am extremely grateful. She has maintained what we built but has already taken it to a greater level. She has the abilities and character to lead at high levels. I could not have gotten through the last twenty-five years without Pat Morris. He has been that high-trust work friend born out of years of difficult and precious circumstances. And nothing can take away my appreciation for Kim Williams. She was my partner from the beginning in reaching for our mutual vision to rebuild and then unify the veterinary departments. Jeanette Fuller, longtime veterinary technician turned hospital manager, has a heart for serving others and helped me in ways I probably still have not fully discovered. Four veteran clinical veterinarians have been exceptional influences in my life and leadership career. They each have been a part of our teams for twenty-five years or more: Jim Oosterhuis, who originally hired me in 1982, has always recognized the importance of a good bedside manner. Meg Sutherland-Smith, who began her career in San Diego and never looked back, is a dedicated clinician, skillful leader, and mentor to many. I recognized very early on that she had an authentic combination of curiosity and drive that destined her for success. Jack Allen has been a four-decade-long friend and colleague and saved the day in South Africa with the simple words, "Make a list." And Jeff Zuba is a genuinely caring man who values good leadership and strives to improve himself and the practice. There are two veterinary pathologists, although not part of my teams, who also deserve special thanks. Bruce Rideout has long served as my sounding board and an example of high personal standards. Linda Lowenstine has helped me and our entire organization many times and in many ways with her incredible knowledge, practical wisdom, and warm friendship.

I thank David Wildt and Susie Ellis who, by extending trust to me, gave me an opportunity to work with them and our Chinese colleagues on the Giant Panda Biomedical Survey, the most significant conservation activity of my career. Over the three years of that survey, they became close travel companions, friends, and wonderful examples of how servant leadership can work well in an unfamiliar culture.

I thank my colleagues Lance Miller and Greg Vicino who, along with many others, educated me about animal welfare as a science. These two were my partners in developing our program at San Diego Zoo Global. They understand that training in leadership skills is crucial for a welfare program to be successful and graciously included me as a trainer in their evidence-based animal welfare management course.

For over ten years, I was a proud member of the San Diego Zoo Global executive team. At eight o'clock every Thursday morning, I watched as the level of trust, the collaboration between members, and our effectiveness as a team—as well as my sincere fondness for them as individuals—grew. I saw the organization prosper through their work. Without exception, each member was gifted and capable in his or her areas of expertise and had a strong desire to see the organization thrive. I thank them for our shared experience. At the time of my retirement, they included Allison Alberts, Beth Branning, Paula Brock, Robert Erhardt, Dwight Scott, Bob McClure, Ted Molter, Tim Mulligan, Mick Musella, Doug Myers, Mark Stuart, and Bob Wiese.

Thanks to my many mentors who helped me in my quest for understanding leadership in the zoo business, especially Art Risser, Werner Heuschele, and Murray Fowler, the men that I mentioned in chapter one as my earliest examples of service-focused leadership. In addition, I was fortunate to have bosses throughout my career who cared for me personally and nurtured me professionally. They included Mitch Bush, Jim Oosterhuis, Art Risser, Bob McClure, and Bob Wiese. I am grateful for their mentorship and support.

I thank Rodney Jackson, who worked with us as an executive coach and people development consultant through the Servant Leadership Institute and remains a valued partner with San Diego Zoo Global. He trained and educated us in practical aspects of leadership and teamwork. He was generous with his encouragement and with background materials used for researching this book.

My praise and sincere gratitude goes to Lynda Stephenson, who was my content editor and coach. She is a real professional who worked hard to put my words, ideas, and stories together in a sensible way. Her knowledge and experience in writing and publishing were indispensable. With her unique combination of creative freethinking and task management skills, she moved me along creatively and kept me on target and on time. Her Texas accent and humor helped us more than once get through tough spots. The pleasant narrative flow and readability are hers. I take responsibility for any lackluster ideas or stories that miss the point. Without her, this book would not have happened.

Thanks most especially to Doug Myers. His belief in the essential need for this project made it a reality. Doug has been the model of the leadership described in this book throughout his career, from his days as the Safari Park's general manager to his current role as CEO of San Diego Zoo Global, leading the institution for nearly one-third of its history. Time and again, I was fortunate to observe his deep, personal humility and his passion to do what is right as a leader. I used his example extensively in this book. By all traditional measures, the organization has thrived under his guidance. More to the point, though, San Diego Zoo Global was reborn under his leadership with an even greater vision for what a great organization can do for conservation and animal life. And he has done all that by caring about people first.

My parents were both a big presence in my life. My mother had a simple and lifelong love for animals, which she passed on to me. My father was a kind and gentle man with a keen intellect, always ready with the right questions to ask. He was the first one to show me that a humble person who can think will exert influence wherever he goes. I have strived my entire life to emulate his way with people. My big brother, Richard, has always been there for me and my family. He looked after me when we were little and that has continued throughout our lives. Now, with our father's character, he leads the family with love and kindness. And I thank my big sister, Shari, for her creative nature, which she so willingly shares with her friends and family. She and I share a love for writing and for the power of words.

My immediate family is of great importance to me. My son, Nicholas, and daughter, Lindy; their spouses, Danielle and Randy; and our grandchildren, Noah, Caleb, Brooklyn, and Macy, are a joy to me and my wife. Nick and Lindy loved and supported my work even when they were little children. They loved to ask me when I came home, "What did you work on today, Daddy?" Throughout their lives, their watchful eyes and listening ears motivated me in the greatest leadership challenge there is—parenting. Despite my trial and error parenting, they have both grown into fine adults, have families of their own, and have made Robin and me proud.

And that brings me to Robin. My greatest thanks to anyone on this earth goes to my wife of forty-two years. She has seen it all and stuck by me. She encouraged me to take every opportunity given to me in my career, even if it made it harder on her. When I became discouraged, she built me up and then never let me take the easy way out when things got rough. She gently pushed me to be a better man and to make a better life for us. She is a quick-witted servant leader who has influence in whatever she does. She has jumped into a surprising variety of roles, from running a day care business to being a vice president of an Internet start-up. She has been my greatest encourager in writing this book and became a taskmaster for setting time for me to work and focus. We love being together as a retired couple. I am most grateful that we could share a faith and a love of the Lord these last twenty years. It has made all the difference. *Soli Deo gloria.*

Appendix 1
Chapter Concepts Review

Chapter 1: The All-Too-Common Story

- Veterinarians are among the most trusted and respected of all professionals, known for their compassion and objectivity.
- Influence is the elusive ability to make an impact on the thinking and actions of others without the need to exert control or authority. Influence springs from a person's value to others.
- Organizational influence is the power to shape policy and affect organizational planning. It can be the catalyst for making the right things happen by cultivating trusting relationships with others.
- Having positional authority does not guarantee influence.
- Veterinarians who rise to positions of leadership tend to understand this: although animals are always the priority, their care must be seen in the context of the broader picture.
- Competence is only part of the equation; character is what sets us apart.
- As the humans are healthy, so is the organization and the animals.
- No one is expendable, even those who don't seem to warrant exceptional treatment.

Chapter 2: Have an Attitude of Service

- True leadership is something that's given and can't be taken away.
- Many veterinary professionals are blind to the fact that others do not see us as we see ourselves.
- Keep this in mind: "It is not about me."
- Servant leadership is not about being nice or overly inclusive.

- Serving others: The animals deserve it. You deserve it.
- Organizational influence grows—starting with an attitude of service.

Chapter 3: Be Humble

- Humility is power under control. True humility involves having authority but choosing not to use it.
- Humility shows strength of character, not weakness.
- Humble leaders have self-confidence, not self-importance.
- Being humble represents an honest approach to reality, an acknowledgment that we are not more important than other people.
- Humility allows us to share credit for successes.
- Humility is a leadership attribute that can be developed.
- Humility is an attractive character trait; humble leaders are likable.
- Humble leaders will change focus, listen, learn, and serve the organization as a whole.

Chapter 4: Put Relationships before Results

- Put your attention first on the people and the results will follow.
- Focus on the people and not the problem. Good leaders need to demonstrate to their team members that their well-being is a higher priority than the situation at hand.
- Leaders remember that while situations are temporary, relationships are long-term.
- Paying attention to people first does not mean avoiding responsibility.
- Putting relationships before results bolsters team trust, influence, and ultimately the health of the entire organization.

Chapter 5: Build Trust

- Trust is among the most fundamental qualities of human

relationships, the glue that holds teams together, creating unity. It is a function of character and competence.

- Trust between coworkers is vital to having successful outcomes for the animals under our care.
- Trust engenders confidence—and a lack of trust leads to suspicion.
- We can, over time, build up "relationship equity" in the "trust accounts" of those around us by the things we do and the choices we make. Animal behaviorists and trainers understand and use this concept of trust accounts.
- Trust takes time and consistency. Trust grows when we extend it to others.

Chapter 6: Prevent and Resolve Conflicts

- Conflict between people who care about animals hurts both the people and the animals in their care.
- Focus on the health of the animals, not on winning an argument.
- There are three key ingredients in preventing a conflict: a servant leader mind-set, trust, and role clarity.
- Talk directly with the other party to resolve a conflict.
- Be prepared for sudden and unexpected conversations that provoke overemotional responses and lead to prolonged conflict.
- Base decisions on evidence, not assumptions.
- The servant leader must stand up for what is right. At the same time, it is entirely possible to advocate for a position without damaging the relationship with the other person.
- Finding the proper balance between inquiring for understanding and advocating our position is a key skill to resolving conflict.
- Leaders must have the courage to speak up when they have a relevant truth that needs to be shared. If you see something important that

others do not, be humble, be kind, be truthful, but be courageous.
- Conflict is best prevented, just like the diseases we fight in our zoo animals and in ourselves.

Chapter 7: Honor Staff and Peers
- Our support staff members will not be secure, loyal, or fully functional unless they understand that we as their leaders care about them and their well-being.
- Honoring those with less authority fosters loyalty and wards off unhealthy conflict.
- People want to be treated with dignity and respect, not just valued for a function they serve.
- A veterinarian, or anyone who is viewed as an authority, is in a unique position to bolster the status of others.
- Honoring others helps to humanize the workplace.

Chapter 8: Connect with Purpose
- Motivating people is a leader's number one job.
- Effective and influential leaders seek to connect with those they lead by fostering a clarity of purpose.
- When people understand and believe in the purpose of their work, they motivate themselves and one another.
- To connect people with purpose, a veterinary leader must always be ready to share the "why" of the moment.
- The "why" gives context and meaning to a procedure or activity. It connects the vision to the task at hand.
- Values answer the "why" question. They give us an idea of who we are. They give us a sense of what ought to be. They tell us where we should be paying attention.

- When we know our values, making decisions is easier.
- Values are strong motivators. It is difficult for people to willingly go against their values. Values dictate decisions and motivate action.

Chapter 9: Give Up Control to Gain Influence

- Pushing for more authority and control usually backfires.
- To gain influence, give up control.
- Successful partnerships are based on establishing clarity. They are not based on equal and identical roles. Rather, they thrive when roles are distinctly defined.
- We can increase our circle of influence regardless of position or title.
- Role clarity is essential. The Decider is the responsible party and has the ultimate decision-making authority. The Adviser influences the Decider. The Adviser can be the primary driver in the decision-making process by initiating dialogue and providing perspective.

Chapter 10: Allow the Team to Develop Standards

- To be most effective, standards should reflect the unique nature and values of each workplace.
- A set of rules, arbitrarily created, can convey that we care more about rules than people.
- Clarity is key. Without clarity, holding people accountable for desired behavior is both difficult and unfair.
- Creating an environment in which everyone takes personal accountability is the most effective way to lead a team in the long run.
- The best approach to encourage personal responsibility is to create behavior-based standards, which inspires a culture in which desired behaviors are identified and consistently practiced.

Chapter 11: Encourage Unity through Diversity

- Every animal functions as a unified body with separate parts that are vital to the whole. When one part doesn't function correctly, the entire animal will be in distress. A successful team is a unified entity made up of individuals who are each vital to the team.
- Diversity itself is a source of strength and unity in a team.
- With a shared purpose, a team benefits from its diverse skills and talents. That establishes unity.
- No matter how significant we think we are, our importance comes only from our collective efforts.
- Gossip is anything negative said about a person to someone who is not able to do anything about it. It is detrimental to the health of a team.
- Being part of a successful and highly functioning team is one of the most satisfying experiences an individual can have.

Chapter 12: Develop Team Members into Leaders

- As zoo professionals, it is our responsibility, and in our best interest, to develop the people around us into leaders.
- We model who we are and what we do every day, filtering this example through our entire staff.
- If we want sustained influence in our organization, we need to invest in others and help those around us to become leaders themselves.
- All people, regardless of rank, should take responsibility and have authority for their area of expertise.
- In an authoritative environment, employees characteristically use language that shows dependence and insecurity.
- We can foster responsibility by encouraging staff members to use phrases that reflect accountability. This method empowers people.
- Focusing on using and improving our strengths is far more effective

than focusing on our weaknesses. Trying to improve our weaknesses requires constant effort with little reward.

- The idea of having a team is to meld strengths so we can be stronger together than apart.
- The three Cs of hiring are character, competence, and chemistry. Character is first on the list because it is the most important.
- The three virtues of hiring are being humble, being hungry, and being people smart.
- Anyone can be a leader, because anyone can serve.

Chapter 13: Develop Yourself into a High-Level Leader

- Looking out for the needs of the organization rather than our own needs requires a broader skill that takes time, training, and intentionality to develop.
- Veterinarians who desire more organizational influence should step out of their role as experts in veterinary medicine and gain experience with broad organizational activities.
- Any zoo veterinarian or other leader offered a chance at being part of executive decision-making needs to obtain basic financial literacy.
- We should use our expertise to benefit the organization and its people.
- One of the greatest values that executives see in veterinarians is their role in animal welfare.
- By working together in partnership, zoo veterinarians, animal welfare scientists, and animal care staff can increase their organizational influence, protect an organization's reputation and assets, and ensure that the animals under their care thrive.
- It takes willingness to work synergistically with other disciplines for this new, potent kind of influential leadership to have its own "opportunity to thrive."

- Good leadership and good animal welfare have a lot in common. The specific needs of the people we lead and the animals we care for may be different, but our responsibility to serve them is the same.

Chapter 14: Look to the Future: Becoming Right Side Up

- For the leaders of the future, becoming board certified is not the finish line. Becoming a successful zoo veterinarian requires more than that.
- Being a career clinician is a noble choice, if that is your desire. Zoos need dedicated, experienced, and wise career clinicians. In this case, leadership skills will still be valuable for effective communication and relationship building.
- Our profession is gaining momentum toward understanding the importance of influence at a higher organizational level. The new generation is realizing that only a lack of leadership skills, more than a lack of technical skills, will limit our profession's impact and influence.
- A different kind of leadership is the right-side-up way to grow influence. Leadership done through service to others is satisfying and exhilarating. It is the road less traveled because it takes more effort and goes against the prevailing leadership wisdom. But the road delivers us where we want to be—where people matter and animals thrive.
- Anyone can be an influential leader regardless of position. An individual can have immense influence without authority. But individuals must step out to earn the right to have broad organizational influence. They must be willing to broaden their perspective to care about the health of the entire organization.
- The path is clear: serving others. The destination is reachable: broad influence to stand up boldly for what is good.
- How we lead and influence others becomes our reputation and a measure of our career success and significance.

Appendix 2
Chapter Discussion Questions

Chapter 1: The All-Too-Common Story

1. How might you or your profession be perceived differently from how you see yourself? Why do you think that might be?

2. What is the expected career path for your profession? Does that path include intentional character development as well as technical training?

3. If you or your team were to lose organizational influence, what would the loss do to your organization? What would the loss do to you personally?

4. In what ways could you broaden your knowledge of your organization to increase your overall influence?

5. What is your first reaction to the phrase "servant leader"? Why might it work in your situation? Why might it not work?

6. Who were (or are) your leadership mentors? In what ways did they excel? In what ways did they fall short? What were the greatest leadership lessons you learned from those mentors?

Chapter 2: Have an Attitude of Service

1. How important is it to have authority to get people to do what you want?

2. What are some possible reasons that senior executives often do not fully appreciate the value of their highly trained and educated professionals?

3. Have you ever worked with someone who was clearly a leader but

had no position of authority? What led people to follow that person?

4. Answer these questions honestly: Do I want to serve myself or others? Where is my focus?

5. What is your measure of being a successful leader?

6. How can you as a servant leader avoid having others take advantage of you?

Chapter 3: Be Humble

1. How is humility a sign of courage rather than weakness? Give examples.

2. Do you think a person can learn to be humble? What would that process look like?

3. What behaviors reveal a person with humble character?

4. Why are humble people so likeable and attractive?

5. Of the best leaders you know personally, which ones would you classify as humble? Which ones have you most enjoyed working with?

Chapter 4: Put Relationships before Results

1. In this chapter, the author advises, "In a crisis, focus first on the people." How would you apply that advice to a medical emergency in which you oversee the procedure?

2. How would you respond to the criticism that putting people before results means avoiding responsibility and validating poor performance? In what ways could that criticism be valid? How could you prevent these things from happening?

Chapter 5: Build Trust

1. Think of a coworker or a friend with whom you have a high trust relationship. What assumptions do you make about that person's

motives toward you and your interests? How does that translate into your getting things done?

2. What are some ways you have built up "relationship equity" in your "trust accounts" with other people?

3. What are the similarities and the differences between trusting relationships that involve people? What about those that involve animals and people?

4. How does the importance of trust differ in various cultures?

Chapter 6: Prevent and Resolve Conflicts

1. How have you seen conflicts between people affect the work they do? What effect does workplace conflict have on animals and people?

2. How do disputes over roles and responsibilities create conflict?

3. What are the differences between avoiding and preventing conflict? Why is one desirable and the other not?

4. What are some ways to prevent conflict from developing?

5. What are some ways to resolve conflicts that develop?

6. What are some of the reasons you might avoid talking to someone directly about a conflict? How can you overcome those fears?

7. What are some important considerations when preparing for a sudden and critical conversation? How can this type of preparation prevent a conversation from turning into a conflict?

8. What causes you to avoid speaking up when you know that something needs to be said? How can you be confident in your choice (whether you speak up or stay silent)?

9. For those things that need to be said, how can you say them in a way that will reduce the risk of creating an unhealthy conflict?

Chapter 7: Honor Staff and Peers

1. What are the practical differences between honoring people and holding them accountable?
2. What does honoring others unconditionally mean to you?
3. Think of a time someone honored you for who you are and not just your job function. What did that person say or do? How did that make you feel?
4. What person do you have an opportunity to honor? What actions can you take to honor that person?

Chapter 8: Connect with Purpose

1. What is the most effective way for someone to motivate you at your highest level?
2. What are some ways that you could share the "why" of the moment?
3. How can you keep the "why" front and center in the decision-making process—particularly when you have to juggle complex and dynamic issues?
4. Write down your personal values as they relate to your work. Are they well aligned with those of the organization? If not, why?
5. Have you observed situations in which people's values were mis-aligned? If so, what was the effect of that misalignment?
6. Do you work with individuals who are high performers and whose values are highly aligned? How do you honor and encourage them?

Chapter 9: Give Up Control to Gain Influence

1. Why would giving up control of a decision be viewed as weak lead-ership? Why is it not?
2. What is the rationale for gaining influence by giving up control?

What is it about human nature that makes this method work?

3. Is it more important to you to have broad, long-term organizational influence or immediate control over important decisions? Why?

4. Is your circle of influence close to the size of your circle of concern? What specific actions could you take to make those circles closer in size?

5. What are the characteristics of the Decider role? What makes it a hard job?

6. What are the characteristics of the Adviser role? What makes that a difficult job?

7. What are the key decision areas in your work? Who shares responsibility with you for making those decisions? In which area are you the Decider? In which area are you the Adviser?

8. Think of a recent example in which you were not the Decider but could have driven the decision as the Adviser. How would you have presented the information to the Decider?

Chapter 10: Allow the Team to Develop Standards

1. What are some unique characteristics of your workplace? What should you consider as you create behavioral standards?

2. As an exercise for yourself or with others, identify organizational values that could be used to drive your standards. What standards might come from those values?

3. How could you involve your entire staff in creating behavioral standards to gain buy-in and establish self-enforced personal accountability?

4. How can you keep people accountable and still serve their needs? How can you uphold high standards without damaging relationships?

5. What are some ways you can use behavioral standards beyond the primary purpose of holding people accountable in a clear and equitable way?

Chapter 11: Encourage Unity through Diversity

1. Unity of purpose and diversity of talents work together to create a strong team. In what ways have you seen that sense of teamwork become damaged?
2. Why might veterinarians be prone to thinking that they are more valuable than other team members? What is wrong with that thinking?
3. How should you respond to someone who gossips to you?
4. Why do you think many zoo leaders see veterinarians and their staffs as highly trained technical experts with diverse talents but separated from the organization as a whole? How could you help to change that perception?

Chapter 12: Develop Team Members into Leaders

1. How can you as a leader make it safe for those around you to find and correct errors?
2. In your authority role, do you feel at all threatened if others take charge of their area of expertise? If so, why? How can you change that response?
3. What are some advantages and disadvantages of empowering employees to be authoritative and make decisions in their areas of expertise?
4. What are some words or phrases that you have found to be helpful in empowering people and building confidence?
5. Think of someone who has unpleasant or negative behaviors in the

workplace. What strengths could you focus on instead that might secondarily deal with the undesirable behaviors?

6. When you hire a new staff member, you impact your existing culture. What characteristics of your culture do you most want to protect?

7. What are some behavior-based interview questions you could ask that would reveal a candidate's degree of humility?

Chapter 13: Develop Yourself into a High-Level Leader

1. What are four important considerations for those preparing for high-level leadership positions?

2. How can you partner with other disciplines to broaden your organizational influence as a high-level leader?

3. What professional attributes can you offer your partners to add value to the relationship?

4. By working together in partnership, zoo veterinarians, animal welfare scientists, and animal care staff can gain the organizational influence necessary to ensure that the animals under their care thrive. What is the ultimate outcome you want to influence? How can working with others help you achieve influence at a high level?

Chapter 14: Look to the Future: Becoming Right Side Up

1. What legacy would you like to leave at the end of your career?

Appendix 3
Chapter Notes and Annotated Reading List

Chapter 1: The All-Too-Common Story

Shanafelt, Tait D., MD, and John H. Noseworthy, MD, CEO. "Executive
Leadership and Physician Well-being: Nine Organizational Strategies
to Promote Engagement and Reduce Burnout." *Mayo Clinic Proceedings* 92, no. 1 (January 2017): 129–46.

This article provides a model for any technical profession that reports
to executive leadership. The key point is the impact that physician burnout and disengagement have on patient care. It is likely a similar dynamic
between veterinarian engagement and animal health care.

Chapter 2: Have an Attitude of Service

Blanchard, Ken. "Servant Leadership." In *Leading at a Higher Level:
Blanchard on Leadership and Creating High Performing Organizations*,
249–76. Upper Saddle River, NJ: Prentice Hall, 2007.

Ken Blanchard is a prolific author and spokesperson for servant leadership. This particular chapter explains the concept and counters the argu-
ments against it.

Greenleaf, Robert K. *Servant Leadership: A Journey into the Nature of
Legitimate Power and Greatness*. 25th Anniversary Edition. Mahwah,
NJ: Paulist Press, 2002.

Robert Greenleaf coined the phrase "servant leadership" in the 1970s. In the book, he describes how someone not in a leadership role can become the leader of a group by serving its members. He provides the classic definitions of servant leadership and offers his ideas on how to measure it.

Chapter 3: Be Humble

Collins, Jim. *Good to Great: Why Some Companies Make the Leap and Others Don't*. New York: HarperBusiness, 2001.

This is a classic book that bases its conclusion on in-depth research comparing good to great companies. I used this reference primarily to highlight the value of humility in leadership. Collins refers to the highest-level leaders (level 5) as having strong personal humility combined with fierce resolve. These were the CEOs who led their companies to greatness.

Hayes, Merwyn A., and Michael D. Comer. *Start with Humility: Lessons from America's Quiet CEOs on How to Build Trust and Inspire Followers*. Westfield, IN: Greenleaf Center, 2016.

This is a little-known book that focuses on the value of humility in the workplace. It uses examples of successful CEOs whose humility was key to their success.

Chapter 4: Put Relationships before Results

Arbinger Institute. *Leadership and Self-Deception: Getting Out of the Box*. San Francisco: Berrett-Koehler Publishers, 2010.

This book is written as a clever story. It talks about how we put ourselves into "boxes" of self-deception by treating others as objects rather than as people with emotions, troubles, and complicated lives (like our own). This concept applies to interpersonal relationships in all walks of life.

Covey, Stephen M. R. *The Speed of Trust: The One Thing That Changes Everything.* New York: Simon & Schuster, 2008.

I used the concepts from this book extensively in my writing about trust and the importance of relationships to get results. Covey quantifies the value of trust in companies and makes a good case for paying attention to relationships to achieve good results in a business. Zoo veterinarians have to rely on trust to gain influence in their organizations.

Grand, J. A., J. W. Lloyd, D. R. Ilgen, S. Abood, and I. M. Sohnea. "A Measure of and Predictors for Veterinarian Trust Developed with Veterinary Students in a Simulated Companion Animal Practice." *Journal of the American Veterinary Medical Association* (JAVMA) 242, no. 3 (February 1, 2013): 322–34.

This paper uses an interesting simulation model to measure the value of trust in a patient-client relationship. The article gives great insight into the topic of trust. It also identifies the specific attributes veterinarians who develop high trust relationships possess.

Chapter 5: Build Trust

Covey, Stephen M. R. *The Speed of Trust: The One Thing That Changes Everything.* New York: Simon & Schuster, 2008.

See annotation in chapter four.

Grand, J. A., J. W. Lloyd, D. R. Ilgen, S. Abood, and I. M. Sohnea. "A Measure of and Predictors for Veterinarian Trust Developed with Veterinary Students in a Simulated Companion Animal Practice." *Journal of the American Veterinary Medical Association* (JAVMA) 242, no. 3 (February 1, 2013): 322–34.

See annotation in chapter four.

Lencioni, Patrick. *The Five Dysfunctions of a Team: A Leadership Fable.* San Francisco: Jossey-Bass, 2002.

This book, like most of his others, is written in the form of clever stories that illustrate his point. Lencioni also puts a lot of attention on trust as a foundation for successful teams.

Chapter 6: Prevent and Resolve Conflicts

Lencioni, Patrick. *The Ideal Team Player: How to Recognize and Cultivate the Three Essential Virtues.* San Francisco: Jossey-Bass, 2016.

This book is in a story format, but it has great practical value for identifying people who will be effective team players. Lencioni uses this strategy for hiring and developing employees in his own consulting business. He looks for people who are humble, hungry (work ethic), and smart (interpersonal skills and self-awareness).

Patterson, Kerry, and Joseph Grenny. *Crucial Conversations: Tools for Talking When Stakes Are High.* 2nd ed. New York: McGraw-Hill, 2012.

This is a useful book for understanding how crucial conversations can develop. These conversations can make a lasting difference in relationships and usually occur suddenly and without warning. The authors give detailed advice on how to recognize and respond constructively to these situations.

"The Ladder of Inference" referred to in this chapter was created by business theorist, organizational psychologist, and Harvard Business School professor Chris Argyris to visualize how we draw conclusions.

Chapter 7: Honor Staff and Peers

Bradley, V., S. Liddle, R. Shaw, E. Savage, R. Rabbitts, C. Trim, L. A. Lasoye, and B. C. Whitelaw. "Sticks and Stones: Investigating Rude, Dismissive, and Aggressive Communication between Doctors." *Clinical Medicine* 15, no 6 (2015): 541–45.

This article demonstrates the damaging effects of certain behaviors not uncommon to doctors (and likely seen in veterinarians and other technical professionals). The destructive behaviors affect patient care and staff morale. The authors discovered that some specialties had a culture that encouraged these behaviors.

Chapter 8: Connect with Purpose

Sinek, Simon. *Start with Why: How Great Leaders Inspire Everyone to Take Action*. New York: Portfolio, 2009.

This book takes a simple concept—the golden circle in which the "why" is the center—and offers profound insights about what is important. The "why" represents the purpose of an enterprise and is the key to motivating employees.

Chapter 9: Give Up Control to Gain Influence

Covey, Stephen M. R. *The 7 Habits of Highly Effective People: Powerful Lessons in Personal Change.* New York: Simon & Schuster, 2004.

This is a classic leadership book with many applications, and I used it in so many ways in my writing. The concept of the "circle of influence" is developed in detail in this book.

Wildt, D. E., A. Zhang, H. Zhang, D. Janssen, and S. Ellis. *Giant Pandas: Biology, Veterinary Medicine, and Management.* Cambridge: Cambridge University Press, 2006.

This book documents the three-year biomedical study on giant pandas in China, describing how the need to understand and accommodate other cultures is vital for developing trusting relationships. Chapter two in particular describes the value of working together across cultures and disciplines. It lists six rules the authors used to address species-based problems when working cross-culturally.

Chapter 10: Allow the Team to Develop Standards

Asch, Sandy, and Tim Mulligan. *Roar: How to Build a Resilient Organization the World-Famous San Diego Zoo Way.* Jersey City, NJ: Highpoint Executive Publishing, 2016.

This is a book about San Diego Zoo Global leadership style. I reference it because it refers to the code of conduct that was used as the basis for our behavior-based standards.

Chapter 11: Encourage Unity through Diversity

Sinek, Simon. *Leaders Eat Last: Why Some Teams Pull Together and Others Don't*. New York: Penguin, 2014.

This is an important book that puts many principles together about the value of servant leadership in team success. Sinek uses military examples, as unlikely as they might seem, to show how leaders should serve rather than be served—i.e., "leaders eat last." This method of leadership is even more important during the crisis of battle than it is during peaceful exercises.

Chapter 12: Develop Team Members into Leaders

Hybels, Bill. "The Three Cs." In *Leadership Axioms: Powerful Leadership Proverbs*, chap. 21. Grand Rapids, MI: Zondervan, 2008.

This chapter summarizes the well-known concept of the three Cs used in hiring. It makes the point that carefully assessing character and chemistry is as important as evaluating a candidate for competence.

Lencioni, Patrick. *The Ideal Team Player: How to Recognize and Cultivate the Three Essential Virtues*. San Francisco: Jossey-Bass, 2016.

See annotation in chapter six.

Marquet, L. David. *Turn the Ship Around! A True Story of Turning Followers into Leaders*. New York: Penguin, 2013.

This is an amazing story of how a nuclear submarine captain learned to be a servant leader (although he did not call it that) to survive being put in charge of an unfamiliar ship at the last minute. In explaining how he developed leaders among his staff, he invented the phrase "I intend to . . ." in place of the more familiar phrase in the navy, "I request permission to . . ." This empowering phrase literally turned the ship around.

Rath, Tom. *StrengthsFinders 2.0.* Washington, DC: Gallup Press, 2007.

This book emphasizes developing oneself and others by improving strengths rather than focusing on weaknesses. It is solidly based on research. Purchase of the book allows the reader to take a strengths-based assessment. It's useful to do as a team to understand complementary strengths.

Appendix 4
Behavioral Standards: San Diego Zoo Global Animal Health

Purpose: To have an exceptionally strong and winning team, the Nutritional Services, Clinical Laboratories, and Veterinary Services departments agree to create and encourage a culture in which we consistently practice the following behaviors.

Format: Each standard starts with one of San Diego Zoo Global's "Rules of Engagement," followed by a catchphrase, an explanatory sentence, and finally a set of clarifying questions to identify specific desirable behaviors.

1. Use Your Words Wisely

Think before you speak.

My words and nonverbal messages affect those around me and our work environment.

Am I being respectful?

- How are others hearing my words?
- Am I being empathetic?
- Am I sending nonverbal messages that might cause misunderstanding?
- Am I addressing the issue directly with the person involved?
- Am I delivering my message in an appropriate manner?
- Am I phrasing my comment in a positive way?
- Am I offering solutions?
- Am I criticizing, condemning, or complaining?
- Is this something I would say if the other person were here?

- Is now the best time to bring this up?
- How am I impacting the other person's day?
- Am I expressing appreciation whenever possible?

2. Be Accountable

Take responsibility.

By holding myself accountable for my actions, there is no one else to blame.

Am I taking action when I see things that need to be done?

- Am I taking full ownership and responsibility for my actions?
- Am I doing what I say I am going to do?
- Am I open to constructive criticism?
- Am I blaming others?
- Am I able to forgive and move on?
- Am I disciplined in my work practices?
- Am I a committed and reliable team member?
- Am I doing what I can to make the organization better?
- Am I meeting my coworkers' and supervisor's needs?
- Am I supporting the team?
- Am I asking for help when I need it?

3. Focus

Work effectively.

When I use my time wisely, the entire workplace can benefit.

Am I prioritizing my day with consideration for the group?

- Am I working on the important task of the day?
- Am I prioritizing my work on a daily basis?
- Am I being considerate of other people's focus?

- Do I work efficiently through tasks by creating my own deadlines?
- Am I respecting and upholding deadlines put forth by others?
- When I cannot be interrupted, am I kind and respectful in the way I let coworkers know?
- Do I have a disciplined technique for handling email?
- Am I aligning with others in my focused efforts?

4. Mine the Gold

Build excellence.

Bring out the best in yourself and others.

Am I empowering others during my day?

- Am I striving to improve?
- Am I recognizing and expressing my appreciation for greatness in others?
- Am I helping others to succeed?
- Am I acting and performing my job duties in a professional manner?
- Am I committed to excellence?
- Am I sharing my knowledge and skills with others?
- How can I become more engaged and excited about my work?
- Am I giving people opportunities to utilize their individual strengths?

5. Strive for Balance

Harmonize.

I can achieve harmony when I balance my work and personal priorities.

Am I taking time to appreciate what I have?

- What work/life imbalances are affecting my performance or interactions with others?

- What am I doing to improve my work/life balance?
- What am I doing to balance the priorities of the department and my own work?
- Can I do something to help others with work/life balance?
- Am I letting go of my personal issues when I am at work?

6. Lighten Up

Joy in the workplace can relieve stress.

I can help to create a pleasant and respectful workplace.

Am I greeting people I come across during my day with a smile and a pleasant greeting?

- Am I "lightening up" and not making mountains out of molehills?
- Is my humor being misinterpreted or offending anyone?
- Am I practicing mindfulness—choosing to be happy and grateful in the moment?
- When appropriate, am I offering light humor throughout the day?
- Am I able to laugh at myself?
- Am I being overly critical of others?
- Am I able to forgive others who have offended me?
- Am I choosing to be positive?

7. Go for the Roar

Make lasting memories.

Create a legacy of learning, innovation, service, and leadership.

Am I making a difference?

- Am I seeking innovative solutions to problems?
- Am I contributing to the influence and reputation of our animal

health team?

- Am I continuing to learn and grow?
- Am I practicing and growing the servant leadership philosophy?
- Am I creating professional benchmarks that exemplify "the roar"?
- Am I providing quality service for our stakeholders?
- Am I building healthy relationships?
- Am I working in a way to ensure that I can rejoice as I look back on my career?

Appendix 5
Servant Leadership Tips

Topic or Situation	What to Say/ How to Act	What Not to Say/ How Not to Act
Key Concept	Putting others' legitimate needs (as opposed to wants) before my own	Insisting on my rights, authority, and privileges
Keep Focus On	Others	Myself
Example Phrases	"What can I do for you?" "How can I help you?" "I don't know, but let me find out for you." "What do you think?" "Let me make sure I understand."	"I don't have time for that now." "That's not my problem." "I have no idea." "This is how we are going to do it." "That's your opinion."
Who We Are	Zoo animal health professionals hired to serve the organization Part of the animal care team	Individuals with rights Highly educated experts deserving respect because of our positions The ones who really know what is best for the animals
Who We Serve	Others over myself People we work with Animals and animal care Whole organization Profession Conservation	Myself over others My department over others My work location
When Things Go Well	Give credit to others Celebrate as a success for the organization	Take credit for myself or my department Say how it could have been so much better

When Things Go Wrong	Take responsibility for the problem Work with others to correct the problem Assume good motives of others	Avoid responsibility Assign blame Gossip Assume bad motives of others
Saying No	Say no to others if not consistent with a strategic priority Say no if not fiscally responsible Say no but . . . Offer to help find other ways to fulfill their needs if I can't	Say no to others so I can control my time Say no so others won't take advantage of me Don't respond at all, just avoid
When Confronted with a Situation in Which You Disagree	Listen for understanding Make efforts to educate Propose alternatives Work for consensus State opposition and then help it become a success	Tell them why it won't work Talk to others about why it's wrong (gossip) Assume/accuse of bad motives Create obstacles to success
Results and Relationships	Developing good working relationships is key to achieving good results	Achieving good results is more important than anything else, even at the expense of others
Needs of Others	Seek to understand others' needs first	Make sure others understand my needs first

Feeding Mikini the okapi a carrot, 2018.

About the Author
Donald L. Janssen, DVM, Diplomate, ACZM

Don Janssen served San Diego Zoo Global as Corporate Director, Animal Health and oversaw the departments of Veterinary Services and Nutritional Services for the San Diego Zoo and the San Diego Zoo Safari Park before he retired in 2016. In his role, Janssen led a staff of veterinarians, nutritionists, technicians, and hospital keepers seeing to the health and well-being of the collection of more than seven thousand animals.

Janssen joined the Wild Animal Park (now called the Safari Park) as an associate veterinarian in 1982, following two years at the National Zoo Park in Washington, DC. Previously, he served a two-year internship and residency at the San Diego Zoo.

He received his undergraduate and graduate training at the University of California, Davis, earning a bachelor of science degree in wildlife and fisheries biology in 1974 and a doctor of veterinary medicine degree in 1978.

Janssen has received numerous awards and research grants and participated in several field projects that took him on expeditions throughout the world. He has authored or contributed to some fifty publications and has made numerous scientific presentations. He was given the Emil P. Dolensek Award in 2009 and the Lifetime Achievement Award in 2017 by the American Association of Zoo Veterinarians.

With Karen the orangutan after her open-heart surgery in 1994.

He received the Alumni Achievement Award from the School of Veterinary Medicine, University of California, Davis in 2015. He is a member of the American Veterinary Medical Association and a member and past president of both the American Association of Zoo Veterinarians and the American College of Zoological Medicine. He is also a member of the Association of Zoos and Aquariums and the former chair of the Animal Health Committee.

About San Diego Zoo Global

San Diego Zoo Global (SDZG) is committed to leading the fight against extinction on behalf of our planet's imperiled animal and plant species. As the world's premier nonprofit zoological organization, SDZG operates three campuses: the San Diego Zoo, the San Diego Zoo Safari Park, and the San Diego Zoo Institute for Conservation Research.

The Zoo, located in Balboa Park, is a safe haven for more than 3,500 threatened and endangered species. The Safari Park is an 1,800-acre wildlife sanctuary, located 30 miles north of the Zoo, where many of Earth's rarest animals roam in expansive habitats. Both parks have renowned botanical collections that together include nearly 30,000 species of plants. The combined attendance of the Zoo and Safari Park is five million visitors each year.

The San Diego Zoo Institute for Conservation Research is the largest zoo-based multidisciplinary conservation science center in the world. The team, which works with 300 conservation partners, is involved with more than 140 projects in 35 countries on six continents. Successes include helping to reintroduce 43 rare animal species—such as the California condor, greater one-horned rhinoceros, harpy eagle, and Grand Cayman blue iguana—back into the wild.

For more information visit: **sandiegozooglobal.org**